Profiting from Services and Solutions

Profiting from Services and Solutions

What Product-Centric Firms Need to Know

Valarie A. Zeithaml, Stephen W. Brown,
Mary Jo Bitner, and Jim Salas

CENTER *for* SERVICES
LEADERSHIP

W. P. CAREY
SCHOOL *of* BUSINESS
ARIZONA STATE UNIVERSITY

Profiting From Services and Solutions: What Product-Centric Firms Need to Know

Copyright © Business Expert Press, LLC, 2014.

The Center for Services Leadership (CSL) is a research center within the W. P. Carey School of Business at Arizona State University (ASU) and an outreach arm from ASU to the business community and the global academic community. The CSL has established itself as a globally recognized authority on how to compete strategically through the profitable use of services.

First published in 2014 by
Business Expert Press, LLC
222 East 46th Street, New York, NY 10017
www.businessexpertpress.com

ISBN-13: 978-1-60649-748-7 (paperback)
ISBN-13: 978-1-60649-749-4 (e-book)

Business Expert Press Service Systems and Innovations in Business and Society Collection

Collection ISSN: 2326-2664 (print)
Collection ISSN: 2326-2699 (electronic)

Cover and interior design by Exeter Premedia Services Private Ltd., Chennai, India

First edition: 2014

10 9 8 7 6 5 4 3 2 1

Printed in the United States of America.

We dedicate this book to the business leaders, managers in the field, scholars, teachers, and students who have heeded the call of service infusion and have shed light on the journey toward solutions and service infusion success. We wish to thank our development editor, Kirsten D. Sandberg, for her quality counsel and enhancements to the book's contents and readability, and administrative assistant, Diane Davis, for her many conscientious contributions in getting the manuscript ready for publication.

Abstract

Designed for executives in companies that manufacture or sell products, this book outlines the challenges of launching a service and solutions business within a product-oriented organization. The target audience—manufacturers, industrial suppliers, technology firms, and other vendors of business goods—views services and solutions as a means to financial growth, reduced revenue volatility, greater differentiation from the competition, increased share of customer budget, and improved customer satisfaction, loyalty, and lock-in. The authors visualize the transition from products sold to services rendered and identify the challenges that leaders will face during the transformation. To overcome those challenges, the book shows leaders how to manage change in five areas: corporate structure; corporate culture; organizational metrics of performance, growth and investment; individual skills and talent development; and core competencies of collaboration and customization.

The authors provide a framework—the service infusion continuum—to describe the different types of services and solutions that a product-rich company can offer beyond warranties, call centers, and websites that support customers in their use of products. The further to the right on the continuum, the more complex—that is, customized and integrated—the services and solutions become to support customers in their strategy, operations, and management. While a company's products can anchor some offerings at the right of the continuum, the service contract supports the customer's decision making rather than product functioning. At the far right are integrated product–service solutions, complex and varied bundles of products and services from their own or partner companies' portfolios to solve a client's business problems.

The book synthesizes the findings of academic research and business publications, draws upon the authors' consulting work, and includes the practical experience of managers amid transforming five *Fortune 100* product-centric companies into service businesses. The authors incorporate vivid examples from AT&T, Caterpillar, Cisco, DuPont, GE, Hewlett-Packard, IBM, Ingersoll-Rand, Pearson Education, Rolls Royce, Salesforce.com, Siemens, Sylvania, VWR International, and Xerox.

The book also introduces the service infusion scorecard, a tool for executives to assess their position on the continuum. Each chapter ends with a set of questions that executives can use as prompts for their own thinking and as conversation starters in meetings.

Keywords

business-to-business, change management, classification of services, collaboration, customer centricity, customization, growth through service, integrated product services, integrated solutions, organizational culture, product–service systems, service-centered, service continuum, service design, service infusion, service innovation, service leadership, service marketing, service scorecard, service strategies, service transition, service-oriented, servitization, solutions marketing, solutions

Contents

List of Figures and Tables

Preface

The transformation of IBM from an internationally renowned business machine maker to a globally respected corporate services and solutions company caught the attention of more than a few executives in the business-to-business space. Leaders of product-oriented companies—manufacturers, industrial suppliers, technology firms, and other vendors of business goods—have come to understand the benefits of offering services and solutions to their customers. They view services and solutions as a means to financial growth, reduced revenue volatility, greater differentiation from the competition, increased share of customer budget, improved customer satisfaction, loyalty, and even lock-in. However, before services and solutions have a positive effect on firm value, a company must reach a critical mass in sales, where services and solutions account for 20 to 30 percent of the firm's total sales.[1] Few executives fully grasp the extent to which they must change their organizations in order to reach this critical mass.

How can industrial companies successfully transform their manufacturing business models into model service and solution businesses? How can they steadily shift their revenues from *goods sold* to *services rendered*? How can they visualize this transition and the challenges they will face? This book addresses those questions. It synthesizes the findings of academic research and business publications, draws upon our own consulting work, and includes the practical experience of managers in the midst of transforming five *Fortune 100* product-centric companies into service and solution businesses.

Our ideas speak to the needs of executives in product-oriented companies that are steeped in cultures of product innovation, engineering, and technical prowess as IBM originally was. Our book acknowledges this rich heritage and offers a means of translating it into an appreciation for service and solution development, design, and delivery with the customer in mind. Not surprisingly, our ideas also speak to service providers who operate more like product-oriented companies.

In our research, we looked at the services these companies already provided, either by law or in response to customers and competitors. We labeled these services *entitlements* tied to product purchase; they are table stakes for competing in a particular product market. The more we worked with these companies, the more we found ourselves speaking in terms of service categories beyond entitlements. Everything clicked when we came up with the concept of a service continuum: We put entitlements on the far left side, representing tactical services that influence a customer's decision to buy or ability to use a product, and we placed the more complex and integrated offerings on the far right side, representing strategic services and solutions that enable a customer to grow its business or to fulfill its mission. We chose the word *infusion* to describe the process of adding customer-centered services and solutions (i.e., services on the right side of the continuum) to a product-centric business model (i.e., services on the left side).

In the following pages, we explain why service and solution transitions pose such challenges and how managers can overcome them. Throughout, we call upon our *service infusion continuum* to distinguish types of services and solutions and to explore how companies can infuse more complex and valuable services into their businesses. New ideas and practical discoveries require such conceptual advances. In studying service infusion, we are beginning to identify and explicate its scope, key success factors, and their relationships.[2]

CHAPTER 1

Introduction

Transitioning from Products to Services and Solutions

To thrive, many manufacturers and other product-dominant companies need to distinguish themselves from their competitors. In a recent study, over three-quarters of manufacturing C-level executives said that enhancing services is a key factor for competitiveness, and over half are planning to establish services as a profit center.[1] These executives are not referring to entitlements, that is, product warranties, repair services, and after-sale maintenance. Instead, they are eyeing more advanced and often more profitable services and solutions such as asset management, business process outsourcing, and consulting. These services support the customer's ambitions, whereas entitlements support the product's efficacy.

Opting to transition from product to service and solution strategies frequently requires firms to do more than infuse services and solutions into their existing business models, but to craft whole new relationship-based models. The profits associated with services supporting customers are often larger than those from a company's products or traditional entitlements, especially when the company's products have little differentiation from competitors'.[2] Given their complexity and level of customization, higher level services and solutions are typically more difficult for rivals to copy than products. They also enable companies to understand how their customers make money, attract new clients, and retain existing clients. This intimate knowledge of a customer's operations can provide a firm with competitive leverage; greater responsiveness to shifts in the business cycle; and ideas for new product, service, and solution development. Customers increasingly look to their product suppliers for ways to increase efficiency or generate more revenues—in other words, they look for more services and solutions, not for more products.[3]

As an aerospace executive noted, services often provide a steadier stream of revenue than goods.[4] IBM, for example, holds over $100 billion in multiyear service agreements with its customers—a stable source of revenue that has helped to buoy IBM through tough economic times when customers could not buy new products.

Transitioning to services and solutions requires leadership skills in change management, because product-centric firms face formidable internal impediments. The foremost is culture. Founded by inventors or entrepreneurs with a technical expertise, these companies tend to value their industrial prowess in making great products, achieving economies of scale, and convincing customers of their merit. When they add services or solutions to their value proposition, they often couch them in the context of *supporting products*.

To launch B2B services that *support customers' goals*, these firms must adopt a new logic, one that emphasizes thoughtfully listening to customers and helping them to solve their problems. Adopting this customer logic is a key success factor. For example, industrial safety has long been a core competency of E. I. du Pont de Nemours and Company, a leader in materials science and an expert in handling hazardous materials. When DuPont formed a strategic business unit to develop and deliver services and solutions, it canvassed its existing customers and learned that a major segment in the oil and gas industry needed its safety expertise. So DuPont designed a service offering around its safety practices.[5] This kind of relationship begins before signing the contract and flourishes or deteriorates relative to the value the firm brings to its customer over the term of contract. If the value is great, the customer renews.

Creating value *with*, rather than for, customers is a second key success factor. For decades, SKF (short for SvenskaKullagerFabriken, which means "Swedish Bearings Factory") has been a global manufacturer and seller of industrial bearings. When a bearing breaks on a customer's production line, production stops and the customer can lose a lot of money. By adopting a customer mind set and leveraging information and communications technology on the production line, SKF changed its traditional business model to become a service and solution provider.[6] SKF no longer sells bearings; it collaborates with customers to provide machinery up-time and productivity.

Ingersoll-Rand Inc. also creates value with customers. A manufacturer of heating, ventilating, and air conditioning (HVAC) products ranging from residential units to huge commercial installations, Ingersoll-Rand is creating a new business model under its Trane brand to offer customers a comfortable climate. For some time, Trane has been gathering performance data through sensors embedded in critical components of Trane's HVAC system so that it can diagnose ahead of time when oil or bearings are wearing down, when filters need changing, and when the system requires maintenance. More recently, Trane Intelligent Systems started using these data to adjust the climate within buildings throughout the day and optimize the equipment's energy use. By transforming HVAC into a service, Trane not only improves its maintenance planning, which reduces its costs but also helps its customers to save energy.[7]

Recommending a competitor's service or product over its own offering when appropriate is another key success factor. This brand agnosticism takes time, if it evolves at all, because it requires deep understanding of a competitor's offerings as well as one's own, and a companywide willingness to advocate a rival's offering to a customer. When this advocacy occurs, it builds trust among customers but not necessarily within one's own organization. We consider it the acid test in determining whether a firm has completely embraced the customer-centric logic. The strategic embracing of brand agnosticism was key to IBM's transformation into being a successful services and solutions company.

Firms in the midst of expanding into services and solutions face many questions about the strategies that will lead them to success. Unfortunately, previous studies have yielded no integrating framework for understanding and leading change. Company leaders are left to rely primarily on the memoirs of Lou Gerstner of IBM or Jack Welch of General Electric. But how can companies replicate a Gerstner's or a Welch's success? What makes firms successful in adding new services and solutions in support of their customers? What types of services will be most profitable and fit best with a company's capabilities? What do executives of product-oriented companies need to do strategically *inside* their organizations to infuse services successfully? This book provides direction.

We focus on growing business-to-business services and solutions that go beyond traditional entitlements (e.g., product maintenance, warranties, and installations) and instead partner with customers in providing higher-value services and solutions (e.g., business process outsourcing, managed services, consulting) that support the customer's corporate executives and business unit heads.

CHAPTER 2

The Service Infusion Continuum

General Electric (GE) has always had a huge service business to support its line of industrial products. The corporation holds multiyear service contracts worth over $150 billion and generates over $50 billion in services revenues annually. About three-quarters of GE's industrial earnings come from services tied to maintaining and enhancing GE products.[1]

In recent years, GE has expanded beyond entitlements (e.g., warranties and repairs) that most companies offer to support a customer's use of their products. We have studied the academic and business literature and conducted our own in depth research on this ever-growing set of companies that are, like GE, adding more complex services and solutions to their portfolio of B2B offerings. We have identified key features of the new services added and we have arranged them in broad categories along a continuum, from basic entitlements on the left side and what we believe to be the most complex services and solutions on the right. We describe complexity in terms of the degree to which the overall service contract consists of an integration of offerings that support the customer's top executives and are customized to their unique needs, circumstances, and aspirations. We describe the process of adding these increasingly complex services and solutions as *infusing* them into the company's business model, where each category of service along the continuum presents its own set of challenges to the company's culture, structure, and capabilities, among them the abilities to customize offerings and to collaborate with customers in the design and delivery of more complex services and solutions. Simply put, not all forms of service infusion are the same.

Figure 2.1 shows the service infusion continuum. To the far left are the traditional types of services that product-oriented firms provide to support their products. These entitlements include warranties,

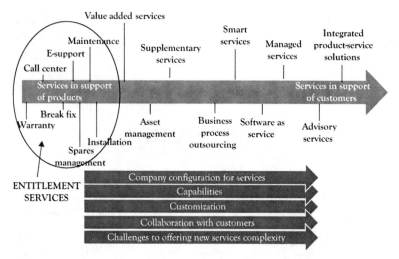

Figure 2.1 The service infusion continuum

call centers, and traditional websites. As we move to the right on the continuum, the company's focus of support shifts from *products sold* to *customers served*. The further to the right on the continuum, the more complex—that is, customized and integrated—the services and solutions become to support customers in their strategy, operations, and management rather than simply in their use of products. Although a company's products can anchor some offerings at the right side of the continuum, as Trane's HVAC components did, the overall service contract supports the customer's decision making rather than merely the product functioning. At the far right are integrated product–service solutions, complex and varied bundles of products and services from their own or partner companies' portfolios to solve a client's business problems.

Services and Solutions Along the Continuum

Entitlements are product-support services, some of which come free with product purchase, such as warranties, call centers, break-fix, online support, routine maintenance, and installation. They enable the initial and ongoing performance of the product, and the company typically offers them at the time products are sold, often bundling them with the product.

These services support products and are the most traditional service offerings in companies. For example, John Deere provides 2000 hours or 12 months of service warranty (whichever occurs first, and within the first 18 months following the date of original shipment) for all of its drivetrain products and for components associated with the product. It provides Deere's customers with the assurance that its products are free from defects in materials and workmanship. If such defects appear within the warranty period, the product will be repaired or replaced by John Deere. Many managers and employees have difficulty imagining services beyond entitlements.

Value-added services provide utility beyond basic product entitlements. These services are ancillary to the core product and can enable the purchase, protection, or usage of the product. For example, Lenovo offers a range of value-added services that extend the initial warranty period of their PCs from one year to five years. They also offer priority technical support that provides direct anytime-access to the right level of tech support on the first call. In addition to financing a PC, Lenovo also offers Accidental Damage Protection that protects against common accidents such as drops, spills, and electrical surges. Value-added services are extra services offered at a modest price or sometimes free in order to forge a stronger relationship with the customer. They can also be fully priced to signal high value. In this case, they represent a revenue or growth stream on a business unit's balance sheet. For example, with its magnetic resonating imaging (MRI) equipment, GE continues to offer training on how to use these complex medical devices.

Asset management is a service typically sold and billed separately from product sales. Service providers have such deep knowledge and experience with the assets they produce that they can assume responsibility for maintaining, deploying, modernizing, and optimizing usage of this asset category (e.g., trucks, cars, or industrial machinery), regardless of whether they manufactured the assets their clients want them to manage. For example, given its expertise in the construction industry, Caterpillar manages the earthmoving equipment that its customers own, regardless of the product brand name. As another example, Xerox offered the City of Riverside, California, a Managed Print Service that allowed Xerox to assume responsibility for managing Riverside's printers and supplies.

The city was able to save $180,000 a year through standardization and central management of their printers.[2]

Supplementary services stem from a company's deep knowledge of its customers' unmet needs and aspirations in an industry sector, build upon the company's expertise in that sector, and stand apart from the company's product revenues in the category. They are typically new stand-alone services that support the client's goals associated with its purchase of the core product. For example, Cisco offers their Software Application Support (SAS) service that supports network-centric software applications by ensuring that these applications remain available, secure, and operate at an optimum performance level. Cisco's SAS service supports over 100 Cisco software application products in major technologies such as security management, network management, mobile wireless, and data center software by keeping them current with the latest application updates. GE offers its Smallworld Water Office solution that provides global data models and a suite of integrated applications that help its utility clients better operate, maintain, and capture diagnostic information for their water supply and drainage network assets. The management of water resources is an important and daunting challenge, especially in the agriculture sector where many municipalities share water resources. TheSmallworld Water Office solution allows customers to document and track their water assets such as water transmission lines, pump stations, drainage networks, and waste-water treatment facilities, to ensure water resources are used efficiently and appropriately.

Business process outsourcing capitalizes on the trend to lower labor costs by outsourcing noncore business processes to companies that excel in those processes and can deliver higher quality for comparatively lower price. Product-oriented firms in the information technology (IT) industry, for example, manage such IT-related processes as application development and quality assurance. Xerox runs back-office processes such as payroll, employee benefits, finance, and accounting. Xerox Revenue Operations, for example, compiles Amtrak's train earnings reports from data submitted by each train's endpoint conductor.[3] Firms also operate front office processes such as customer service (e.g., running call centers and live chats). Some of these outsourced services are provided through remote operations located outside the boundaries of the primary company. As another example, AT&T offers network security services that protect its customers from malicious cyber attacks. Armstrong Coal Company, which specializes in providing custom-blended coal to meet the needs of electric power plants throughout the U.S. Midwest and Southeast, hired AT&T to monitor and manage its network remotely to assure a highly secure environment.

Smart services often depend on sensor technology, where a company embeds sensors into its products and networks them to computers that oversee their functioning. The strategic design and placement of sensor technology make these services possible. They are called smart because powerful computing systems essentially perform the service: they automatically run sophisticated analytics with only modest levels of human interaction.[4] For example, GE and Rolls Royce build sensors into their aircraft engines so that they can monitor these engines remotely to track performance and anticipate problems. This service can detect an engine's wear or need for maintenance. Smart services are primarily pre-emptive rather than reactive or even proactive; computers gather reliable evidence of the need for servicing to avoid problems and to minimize human error.[5] As another example, Caterpillar offers Vital Information Management System (VIMS) that provides operators, service personnel, and managers information on a wide range of vital machine functions. Caterpillar incorporates numerous sensors into their vehicle design that allows VIMS to detect an impeding or abnormal condition in any of the machine's systems and alert the operator, instructing him or her to take appropriate action such as modifying machine operation, notifying the shop of needed maintenance, or performing a safe shutdown of the machine. This improves the availability and extends the life of the machine, while reducing both repair costs and the risk of a catastrophic failure. The sensors attached to products can also spawn new information-based services that are marketed independent of the products. GE, for example, is applying advanced analytics and software to data generated from sensors to develop new service businesses that not only help manage an airline's or railroad's engines, but how fast its planes and trains go and how flight and train schedules are coordinated.

Software as Service enables customers to access the company's proprietary software when needed rather than buy a license for an application and install the software on a client's system. The software provider licenses the application to customers for a single user or group of users on demand, for a given period of time, or pay as you go. The emergence of cloud computing, storage, and services has significantly enhanced opportunities for software as service. For example, Salesforce.com offers its customers a range of cloud-based services that they can utilize for a single monthly fee, per user. Bayer Pharmaceuticals relies on Salesforce.com's cloud-based customer relationship management system to track sales calls, invitations to events, and samples distributed. Bayer uses Salesforce.com to create customized reports and get real-time data to target physicians and cut the time it takes to disseminate meaningful data to sales teams. Norfolk Southern Railroad uses GE Transportation's software and analytical tools to optimize hundreds of train schedules and train speeds. The software service means that more locomotives can use the same rail tracks, move faster, and conserve fuel simultaneously. Norfolk estimates that an increase in its locomotives' speed of just one mile per hour will save it over $200 million in operating and capital expenses annually.

Managed services involve transferring day-to-day management of specific functions to another firm for more effective and efficient operations. For example, both Hewlett Packard and Xerox offer managed print services whereby they assess the client firm's printing needs and existing resources (e.g., printers and printing equipment), offer recommendations on how to save money and gain efficiencies, and then implement these recommendations. They make money based on the ensuing performance of their clients' printing. When a client's needs change, HP or Xerox continues to maintain responsibility for decisions, implementation, and outcomes. This category of services differs from asset management and business process management in that it is more strategic: The company assesses what the client owns and participates in higher-level internal decision making to choose the optimal service. In health care, for example, hospitals tend to be structured in silos where information is misplaced or lost when staff members hand off patients from department to department. GE's Patient Care Capacity Management Solutions enables hospital staff to tag and track patients accurately so that each staff member can deliver better care faster, more cost effectively, and with fewer errors.

Advisory services are professional consulting services and solutions that product-oriented companies offer to high-level directors and executives of client firms to improve managerial practices as well as individual or organizational performance.[6] The professional advice often stems from years of deep experience with the type of equipment the company manufactures. The more a company studies how, where, why, under which circumstances, and to what effect its clients use its equipment, the more guidance it can provide to a larger set of prospective clients. Advisory services help managers improve the practice of management in virtually all areas of a client firm. For example, drawing on over 200 years of experience, DuPont offers Sustainable Solutions to help their clients build safer, more efficient, and more environmentally sustainable business practices. Suncor Energy relied on DuPont to help improve their environmental impact and worker and process safety management systems in the Oil Sands region of Canada. DuPont was able to make a strategic contribution because it had the scale to work with Suncor worldwide to develop programs to improve processes focused on work hazards, safety, incident and change management, and audit and assessment.

Another example involves IBM's consulting proficiency in financial management, human capital management, customer relationship management, people and process transformation, and supply chain management.[7] These services originally formed around the corporation's products sold. However, over time, advisors develop their own expertise and may be hired for that alone. GE has also designed a full suite of health care equipment and software, from MRIs to AgileTrac capacity software that allows GE Healthcare clients to harness the power of Real-Time Location System technology to track the movement of patients throughout their hospital. St. Luke's Episcopal Hospital in Houston, Texas, uses GE Healthcare's advisory services to improve capacity utilization and the patient experience. In the operating room alone, the hospital has increased capacity by 750 patients a year. This increase has reduced each patient's average length of stay by half a day and saved more than $6 million in operating room costs.

Integrated product–service solutions are the most complex type of offering. They are not merely combinations of a company's goods and services, although suppliers often view them this way. Instead, they derive from a company's deep understanding of its customers' unique requirements, such that they can customize, integrate, deploy, and support a package of goods and services, including those offered by competitors.[8] Long-term success depends on the company's ability to collaborate potentially with customers, partners, and competitors in the drafting and execution of such a complex contract. Advisory services are often integral. For example, most airplanes call on three to five different data systems—one for take-off, one for in-flight, one for landing, and so forth—during the course of a flight. Until recently, these data systems could not talk to one another, resulting in fuel inefficiencies. Through acquisitions of other businesses and deployment of its own flight operations expertise, proprietary software, and analytical capabilities, GE Aviation is able to advise customers on how to integrate these data systems and reduce fuel consumption by two to five percent, regardless of whether they use GE aircraft engines and components. By integrating its advisory services with software tools, GE helps customers to reduce some of their costly payload, especially fuel, and add such revenue-producing payload as passengers and cargo. GE Aviation estimates that its integrated services could save the global airline industry annually more than $4 billion in fuel costs, while concurrently eliminating over 12 million metric tons of carbon dioxide emissions. IBM also offers integrated solutions that help its client's migration to cloud-based computing. They work closely with clients to fully understand their requirements for customized plans to take existing production workloads, such as SAP or Oracle applications, and move them to the cloud. Doing so may involve the combination of IBM servers or even products from IBM's competitors to deliver the best solution for the customer. IBM will install and provide ongoing support for the solution. Clients view these types of hybrid solutions from IBM as the beginning of a strategic partnership as opposed to a simple transaction and expect IBM to periodically provide proactive advice and support (Table 2.1). Table 2.1 distinguishes the types of services on the continuum.

Table 2.1 Services on the continuum

Type of Service	Description and Revenue Model	Examples of Phrases Used	Company Illustration
Entitlement services	Services that enable initial and ongoing usage of the product, sometimes offered free as a basic or negotiable term of product sale. Often offered as a service-level agreement contract.	• Call centers • Delivery • Installation • Online support • Repair/maintenance • Warranties	John Deere's drivetrain service warranty.
Value-added services	Service options that provide utility beyond the company's basic product or enable the purchase, protection, or usage of the product. The company might charge a nominal or significant fee, offer the service free for a limited time, or provide it for free as part of the product purchase to increase customer switching costs.	• Credit • Customer service agreements (CSAs) • Extended warranties that lengthen the duration of the standard warranty • Financing • Insurance • Accidental Asset Protection	• AT&T's Audio conferencing services. • Lenovo's extended warranties for their PCs, financing, and accidental damage protection.
Asset management services	Provider assumes responsibility for managing a group of the customer's assets that may include but are not limited to provider's own products. Services rendered are typically sold and billed separately from goods sold.	• Logistics • Maintenance • Safety or security • Software upgrade or protection • Inventory control	• Boeing's maintenance of airplanes, upgrade of onboard computer technology, and safety inspections. • Caterpillar's maintenance of equipment, scheduling, or logistics of equipment deployment; and new operator training. • Xerox's managed print services.

(Continued)

Table 2.1 *Services on the continuum* (Continued)

Type of Service	Description and Revenue Model	Examples of Phrases Used	Company Illustration
Supplementary services	New, stand-alone services that support the client's goals associated with its purchase of assets and have independent revenue streams.	• Feasibility studies • Financing of operations • Insurance of operations • Safety or security of operations • Training of staff • Integration services	Cisco's Software Application Support (SAS) service.
Business process outsourcing	Customers outsource discrete noncore processes to companies that excel in managing those processes at lower cost and with greater quality. They are usually annual or multiyear contracts covering one or more processes, priced according to customer usage or a business outcome.	*Back-office processes* • Accounting • Application management • Employee benefits, payroll • Employee travel • Financial administration • Global process services • IT infrastructure services • IT outsourcing *Customer-facing processes* • Customer call centers • Customer billing or payments • Customer data management	• Paychex payroll and HR services manages the payroll and employee benefits of many small businesses. • Xerox Revenue Operations compiles Amtrak's train earnings reports from data submitted by each train's endpoint conductor. • AT&T's network intrusion detection services.

Smart services	Automated technology-based services that depend on sensors and networks where computers monitor product usage and alert clients or employees to changes that warrant human or machine attention. They are usually annual or multiyear contracts, priced according to number of devices or nodes on the network.	• Data analytics or diagnostics services • Remote monitoring and troubleshooting • Automated systems upgrades • Proactive monitoring • Remote patient monitoring • Machine-to-machine technologies • Remote sensing	• Rolls Royce monitors its aircraft engines remotely to anticipate problems. • Caterpillar's Vital Information Management System.
Software as service	A company provides customers with access to and use of the company's proprietary software on demand, where customers pay per use, pay per user, by subscription, or per other contractual basis.	• Cloud computing • Data storage and backup • Hosting • Mobility • Website security • Software on demand • Virtualization services • Infrastructure as a service • Platform as a service • Centralized computing	• IBM hosted United Nations Development Program's enterprise resource planning system Atlas. • Amazon web services drives UniCredit Bank, NASDAQ OMX, Ericsson, Unilever, Pfizer, Hitachi Systems, the European Space Agency, and the University of Melbourne. • Salesforce.com's customer relationship management (CRM) services.
Managed services	Client transfers strategic management of a particular function to the service provider for improved effective and efficient operations. They are usually annual or multiyear contracts, priced according to the number of devices, tiers of service, value-based, or an a la carte model.	• Accounting and finance • Human resources • Information technology • Import/export and traffic • Procurement and logistics • Supply chain • Intellectual property management • Design and production • Customer service	• Hewlett Packard and Xerox offer managed print services.

(Continued)

Table 2.1 Services on the continuum (Continued)

Type of Service	Description and Revenue Model	Examples of Phrases Used	Company Illustration
Advisory services	Professional consulting services that product-oriented companies offer to high-level executives of client firms to improve managerial practices and individual or organizational performance. They are usually problem focused, although firms can be held on retainer. They are sometimes priced per project with a set number of hours or on an hourly basis.	• Alliances and joint ventures • Application innovation • Business analytics • Business strategy • Smarter commerce • Competitive strategy • Mergers and acquisitions • Leadership development • Consulting services	• DuPont's environmental impact and worker and process safety management services.
Integrated product–service solutions	The most complex type of offering that springs from a company's deep understanding of its customers' unique requirements, such that it can customize, integrate, deploy, and support a package of goods and services, including those offered by competitors and often in collaboration with customers. They are usually annual or multiyear contracts, possibly retainerships. Sometimes priced using a value-based pricing approach, gain sharing, or on a per-project basis.	• Advisory services with software tools • Proprietary software with analytical capabilities • Business solutions • Hybrid solutions • Service solutions	• IBM offers a variety of solutions such as their suite of smarter computing solutions that can take a company's entire IT infrastructure and migrate it into the cloud.

Five Dimensions of Change Across the Continuum

One of our most important messages in developing the service infusion continuum is this: As a firm begins to add offerings in the middle to the right side of the continuum, corporate leaders must manage key internal changes for any new service or solution to succeed over time. Through our research, we identified five key dimensions of change:

- company configuration or structure;
- customer-facing capabilities of sales, delivery, and support;
- customization of offerings;
- collaboration with customers;
- challenges of capital investment, marketing decisions, performance metrics, and partnering with competitors and other supply-chain members.

We refer to these changes collectively as the "five C's," each of which affects the proper design, sale, delivery, and management of services and solutions along the continuum. A second key message is that each type of service along the continuum requires its own changes in terms of the five C's. For example, launching smart services requires a change in product design, manufacturing, and testing, whereas offering software as a service requires a change in corporate IT system access and security. Neither of those requires the extensive cultivation of people skills needed by consultants who will be collaborating with clients and supply chain partners in customizing and deploying integrated services and solutions. For example, HP's Proactive Care Smart Services requires HP to incorporate sensors and network elements into the design of their printers and servers. HubSpot, an all-in-one inbound marketing software company, allows its clients to purchase their solutions on a monthly software license basis, which supports a large array of network services designed for redundancy and survivability so that their customers always have access to their services. Hubspot validates clients through network IDs and passwords, allowing paid users access to their service. In these two examples, the depth of collaboration with the customer and resources required from the service provider differ greatly.

When GE's Commercial Lighting Team develops an integrated product–service solution for a client, they work hand-in-hand with them
to jointly design and create an integrative solution that solves a client's
immediate and long-term goals and objectives. GE consultants advise
and help implement lighting solutions that optimize return on investment and ensure that the solution is integrated seamlessly throughout a
client's existing infrastructure.

OUR RESEARCH

Many services in product-centric companies are service *entitlements*
tied to product purchase—they are table stakes for competing in a
particular product market. In our research working with companies,
however, the we found more companies talking in terms of service
categories beyond entitlements. Everything clicked when we came up
with the concept of a service continuum: We put entitlements on the
far left side, representing tactical services that influence a customer's
decision to buy or the ability to use a product, and we placed the
more complex and integrated offerings on the middle and right side,
representing strategic services and solutions that enable a customer to
grow its business or to fulfill its mission. We chose the word *infusion*
to describe the process of adding customer-centered services (i.e., services on the right side of the continuum) to a product-centric business
model (i.e., services on the left side).

When we talked to companies, we asked the question, What
internal changes do product-oriented firms need to make to offer
these higher-valued services and solutions to their customers? For
the last five years, that question has driven our research, case writing, executive education programs, and corporate consulting. Much
of what we present in this book comes from what we learned from
five *Fortune* 100 corporations in heavy equipment, health care supply, commercial building, aerospace, and diversified manufacturing.
Each company wants to expand into services but appreciates the
challenges.

In each business, we identified a lead executive involved in forming a business unit to provide B2B services and solutions. This executive, in turn, identified four to six other executives or upper-level managers to participate in the study.

In our research, we have focused on the changes required to add services and solutions on the right side of the continuum, because those are the most complex. In this book, we use the terminology that resonated most with research participants, peer reviewers of our published papers, and our clients. How executives describe their offerings internally and to clients often varies, as does where they place their services on our continuum. They blur the lines between types of services and solutions even further.

Our methodology is more fully presented in the Appendix 1.

Table 2.2 provides brief descriptions of the five C's, the overall nature of the changes that leaders should anticipate for each C, and questions they should be asking.

Customization. As a company begins to offer more complex and higher-priced services and solutions in support of customers, customers begin to expect the company to customize those offerings to their unique needs and circumstances.[9] Most of the published research on the customization of services has been conceptual, although several studies are case-based. Several studies of the mass customization of goods describe how companies can develop and combine standardized modules to customize offerings for clients.[10]

Capabilities needed. To infuse services and solutions into their business models, companies need talent with different skills and competencies, and human resources departments that can address the changing HR requirements of service infusion. The more complex the service, the greater the number of customer contacts the supplier will need to develop, and the higher in the organization some of those contacts will need to be. A considerable number of case- and interview-based studies show clearly that sales and delivery people need different skills when a company offers complex services and solutions in addition to

Table 2.2 A snapshot of the five C's

Dimension	Description	Change Across the Continuum	Questions Managers Should Ask
Customization	The organizational ability to tailor offerings to customers' unique needs and circumstances.	As companies move into more complex services in support of customers, there is a greater customer expectation for customization.	Which activities can we standardize? Of those we can standardize, can we replace human activities with technology-based processes? Of those we cannot standardize, can we minimize variation to maintain costs? Can we bundle human activities into processes, packages, or modules? Can we combine technology and people into unique offerings? How much customization can we outsource to the customers themselves?
Capabilities needed	The requisite knowledge and skills of customer-facing staff members and the organization's ability to develop and enhance it.	The more complex the service, the greater the number of customer contacts the supplier firm will need to develop, and the higher in the organization some of those contacts will need to be.	Do our sales people have indepth knowledge of customer's needs and benefits the firm can provide? Are they transaction oriented or relationship oriented? How proficient are they at financial planning? Are they order takers or account managers? Do they think tactically by quarter or strategically over time? Do service delivery people possess both technical proficiency and business acumen?

Company configuration	The company structure that is conducive to service infusion.	The service-oriented firm is usually organized around customers, not products.	How do we deliver entitlements? Can we build upon that service capability or learn from our successes and failures there? Do we have any other success in delivering services in the company? Can we conduct small experiments delivering services through a separate and parallel services unit, as well as through the existing product unit?
Collaboration with customers	The organizational ability to involve customers in generating ideas, designing, developing, producing, delivering, and improving services.	As companies move toward the right side of the continuum, they need to find ways to collaborate more with their customers.	How can we engage customers in —idea generation —new service development —new service design —service delivery —usage of service —feedback on service experience —service improvement How should we act upon what we learn?
Challenges to existing capabilities	Back-office capabilities of capital investment, marketing, performance metrics, and collaboration with competitors and other supply-chain members.	As companies move toward the right on the continuum, they test the limits of skills and tools honed for decision making and action taking around products.	Are our decision-making tools preventing us from seeing and seizing service opportunities? How do we need to adjust capital investment process? What performance metrics are appropriate for services? How do we develop value propositions for new services? How do service pricing strategies differ from product pricing? How should we work with partners in the service space?

or combined with products. These positions must be able to think strategically and in the long term, cultivate customer relationships, manage accounts effectively, master financial planning for services, and connect their indepth and sophisticated knowledge of customers' demands with their understanding of what their company can realistically supply.[11]

Company Configuration. Most goods-oriented firms are organized around products or product categories, and employees focus on their own products and frequently compete for corporate resources, management recognition, and customer attention with employees in other product units. The goods-oriented firm's structure is usually hierarchical, with well-defined levels and layers established over time. The budding service-oriented business unit is usually organized around customers, perhaps separate from or parallel to the company's product units, but sometimes—or over time—integrated with product units. Given the limited and conflicting research, we provide options and considerations rather than strong direction on the structure of service and solution organizations.

Collaboration. To offer more complex and higher-priced services and solutions that support a customer's goals and ambitions, a company must begin to involve customers in generating ideas, designing, developing, producing, and delivering new offerings. The process of customer collaboration goes beyond new service and solution development and delivery through measurement of usage, feedback on the experience, and service improvement or innovation. This broad view of collaboration fits with current defined solutions and research on the value of involving customers in new service development.[12]

Challenges to existing capabilities. As companies move toward the right on the continuum, they will encounter significant challenges in their abilities to invest strategically for services growth, create metrics appropriate for services, develop value propositions and pricing strategies, and work with partners.

Culture. Although not overtly identified in the Service Infusion Continuum, overriding and shaping each of the C's is the mega-C of culture, a demonstrated pattern of shared values within a company. To launch higher-valued services and solutions, executives of product-centric firms must orchestrate profound cultural adjustments not just in corporate structure and capabilities but also in attitudes and beliefs. Employees in product-oriented companies tend to value the technical and engineering prowess embodied in every product. They focus on what they can invent, manufacture, sell in volume, and ship to customers. In contrast, employees of customer-centric organizations tend to value the quality of services and solutions delivered to internal and external customers alike.[13] They look for new ways not just to serve customers but to solve customers' problems better than their competitors can.

A service and solution culture reinforces customer-oriented values (e.g., focus on the customer, treat fellow employees as you would treat customers, think outside our product catalog) and operationalizes those values in performance metrics and incentives. They deploy technology and engineering ingenuity, including that of their competitors, to serve the customer. This cultural shift is, of course, dramatic for many product-oriented corporations.

In the rest of the book, we expand on each of these C's—configuration of the service and solution company (Chapter 3), customer-facing capabilities (Chapter 4), customization capabilities (Chapter 5), collaboration capabilities (Chapter 6), challenges to product-based capabilities (Chapter 7), and cultural change (Chapter 8)—in terms of the managerial issues and approaches that companies take to bring about the necessary change.

The Service Infusion Scorecard

Where does your company operate on the service infusion continuum? Table 2.3 is a scorecard to guide your exploration and discussion among colleagues. You might discover pockets of higher level service and solution innovation across your organization and can learn from their managers' experiences.

Table 2.3 The service infusion scorecard

Category	Inventory
Entitlement services	• Are we offering services that enable initial and ongoing usage of our product, such as any of the following? __ Delivery of product __ Installation __ Warranties __ Call centers __ Repair or maintenance __ Online support or website __ Other?
Value-added services	• Are we offering services that provide utility beyond our basic product or that enable our customers to buy and protect the product? __ Financing __ Credit __ Insurance __ Extended warranties __ Customer service agreements __ Other?
Asset management	• Are we assuming responsibility for managing some of our customer's assets of the type that we manufacture and sell? • Are we responsible for any of the following for a group of assets? __ Maintenance __ Safety or security __ Software upgrade or protection __ Logistics __ Other? • Do these assets include ours and competitors' products?

Supplementary services	• Are we offering services that support our customer's goals independent of any product we sell? For example, do we offer any of these? ___ Financing of operations ___ Insurance of operations ___ Safety or security of operations ___ Feasibility studies ___ Training of staff ___ Other?
Business process outsourcing	• Is our company managing any single business process for our customers? • Back-office processes ___ Compliance ___ Employee benefits ___ Employee travel and expenses ___ Mail or package logistics ___ Network or IT maintenance ___ Payroll ___ Other? Customer-facing processes ___ Billing or payment or collection ___ Call centers ___ Data management or identity protection ___ Other?

(Continued)

Table 2.3 The service infusion scorecard (Continued)

Category	Inventory

Smart services	• Have we embedded sensors into any of our products?
	• Can we work with product teams to embed sensors into more products?
	• Are we offering automated technology-based services that depend on sensors and networks?
	• Are we offering any of these?
	  ___ Remote monitoring
	  ___ Systems upgrades
	  ___ Data analytics or diagnostics
	  ___ Other?
	• Are our computers monitoring product usage and alerting clients or employees to changes that warrant human attention?

Software as service	• Are we providing customers with access to and use of our company's proprietary software?
	• Are we hosting customer-facing application or back-office operations or both?
	• Are we facilitating any of the following?
	  ___ Application management
	  ___ Website security or piracy protection
	  ___ Data backup or archiving
	  ___ Analytical tools
	  ___ Project management or scheduling
	  ___ Conferencing or webinars
	  ___ Other?

Managed services	• Have clients asked us to manage a particular business function for improved efficiency? Any of these?
	___ Supply chain management
	___ Intellectual property management
	___ Financial administration
	___ Accounting
	___ Legal
	___ Public relations or investor relations
	___ Safety or security management
	___ Customer service
	___ Other?
Advisory services	• What deep expertise resides within our company? Do we share it with our customers? How?
	• Are we providing professional consulting or strategic advice to high-level executives in any of these functional areas?
	___ Business analytics and big data ___ Innovation and new product development
	___ Change management ___ Marketing, sales, and service
	___ Customer relationship management ___ Operations and supply chain management
	___ Finance and risk management ___ Strategic planning and implementation
	___ Human resources and talent management ___ Other?
	___ Information technology

(Continued)

Table 2.3 The service infusion scorecard (Continued)

Category	Inventory
Advisory services (continued)	• Are we providing professional consulting or strategic advice in any of these sectors? ___ Advanced electronics ___ Infrastructure ___ Aerospace and defense ___ Insurance ___ Life sciences ___ Automotive and assembly ___ Media and entertainment ___ Banking ___ Metals and mining ___ Chemicals and petroleum ___ Oil and gas ___ Communications ___ Pharmaceuticals and medical products ___ Consumer packaged goods ___ Private equity and principal investors ___ Education ___ Public sector ___ Electric power and natural gas ___ Pulp, paper, and foresting ___ Energy and utilities ___ Retail ___ Financial markets ___ Semiconductors ___ Financial services ___ Social sector ___ Government ___ Telecommunications ___ Health care systems and services ___ Travel, transportation, and logistics ___ High technology ___ Other?
Integrated product–service solutions	• Are we creating product and service platforms for specific customers that we could not offer to other customers without adjustments? • Are we customizing, integrating, and supporting a package of goods and services for customers? • Are we collaborating closely with customers in the design and delivery of any products and services?

Pricing and revenue models	For each of the services or service categories offered, consider these questions:
	• Who designed the value proposition?
	• Who is responsible for maintaining upgrades and innovation, particularly of smart services and software as service?
	• Are we charging a fee for these services or are we offering them free as a basic or negotiable term of product sale?
	• How do we make these pricing decisions? Who set the pricing strategy? Who has pricing decision rights?
	• How are we pricing and billing these services?
	  ___ Annual basis
	  ___ Billed separately from product purchase
	  ___ Bundled with bulk sale
	  ___ Free for a limited time (e.g., promotional pricing)
	  ___ Monthly basis
	  ___ Multiyear contract
	  ___ Nominal fee (e.g., covers cost of provision)
	  ___ On demand, pay per use
	  ___ One-time-only free as part of product purchase (e.g., the blade that comes with the razor)
	  ___ Pay per number of assets
	  ___ Pay per users
	  ___ Other?

Delivery and performance metrics	For each of the services or service categories offered, consider these questions: • Who is responsible for selling these services? • Who is responsible for delivery? • Who sets targets for service revenues? • Who owns the customer relationship? • What are the performance metrics and who tracks them? • On whose budget do the costs appear? • Do the revenues and expenses appear on a separate profit-and-loss statement or are they combined with the P&Ls of other services?

For Executive Discussion

As you consider opportunities to infuse services and solutions into your company, here are some prompts to guide your exploration and conversations. The point is to understand why your company does what it does in terms of services and solutions and to learn from those who preceded you. You might put these questions to your management team and compare your understanding of configuration.

1. Who offers services and solutions in our company? That is, which departments, business units, and divisions offer services to external customers?
2. What kind of services and solutions? Do any of these fall on the right side of the infusion continuum?
3. Are these standalone service and solution organizations or do the product units deliver services tied to the use of their products? Why? How did we initially deliver these services and solutions?
4. How do the roles, responsibilities, decision rights, resources, and rewards of the service personnel differ from those of the product personnel? If no difference, why not?
5. What other kinds of service and solution structures do I see?
   - By country, continent, or other region? Developed or emerging market?
   - By customer type? Public or private; government; not-for-profit?
   - By account size? Small, medium, or large?
   - By business process?
   - By business function?
   - By industry sector?
6. Are we running our service and solution organizations as profit centers with profit and loss responsibility? Why or why not?
7. If we have embedded services and solutions in product units, are managers emphasizing services on par with products and assigning sufficient accountability for service and solution design and delivery on par with product design and manufacturing?

8. How many customer toll-free numbers does our company support? If we have more than one, why? The more numbers, the greater the urgency to restructure.

9. How many customer databases does our company support? If more than one, then do customers appear in more than one database? Why? The more databases and redundancy, the greater the urgency to restructure.

10. Who has access to customer databases and why? Customer by customer, is there one shared view of the whole customer, or a myriad different views, none of which is complete?

11. When delivering services and solutions, how well do we share resources across the firm? Remember, customer knowledge is a resource.

12. How robust are our resource flows, that is, the degree to which various business units access, acquire, or share each other's resources to support the service and solution development and delivery process?

13. How would I describe the service organizations within our company in terms of these design factors?
    - Culture—service and solution orientation of corporate values manifested in employee behavior
    - Personnel—recruitment, training, assessment, and compensation
    - Structure—organizational distinctiveness between product and service or solution businesses, and proximity to customers of the service organization.

14. As we evolve our service operations, how will we need to reorganize away from our product orientation? Do we have opportunities to integrate services and solutions in stages? Might any of the following strategies work?
    - Flattening the organization to localize decision making and remove multiple layers that slow down activities.
    - Increasing resource flows by integrating business unit responsibilities, creating incentives for intra- and interfirm collaboration, and decentralizing decision-making authority so that we can deliver increasingly complex services and solutions on the right side of the continuum.

- Overcoming organizational silos by implementing structural mechanisms and processes that allow employees to focus laser-like on the customer and that harmonize information and activities across units.
- Reorganizing around categories of service rather than by regions or by products.
- Restructuring from front to back and center, where front-end customer-facing units develop, sell, and deliver integrated solutions to customers, back-end product and service units support the front-end through standardized modules of services, and a strategic center mediates between back-end units.

CHAPTER 3

Company Configuration for Services and Solutions

Nearly 20 years ago, Siemens Management Consulting started as a small and independent group with only one offering, IT system solutions.[1] Leveraging its own experience in change management, Siemens expanded to offer change management advice. It set up a matrix organization of three customer groups—industry, financial services, and public services—and two consulting offerings, strategic IT consulting and management consulting. In 1997, Siemens separated financial services into a center of excellence, dedicated to managing financial risks within Siemens and addressing the financing challenges of Siemens and its customers. The IT business struggled to compete with larger competitors such as IBM. In 2010, Siemens sold its IT solutions and services unit for U.S. $1.1 billion to its French rival, Atos Origin SE. It also took a 15 percent stake in Atos and awarded Atos a seven-year outsourcing contract, under which Atos would provide Siemens with managed services and systems integration.[2]

Other Siemens services have flourished across the continuum. For example, Siemens Shared Services LLC is a standalone unit that performs back-office functions that benefit its customers through economies of scale and functional expertise in accounting and finance, human resources, information technology, import or export and traffic, and procurement and logistics. Siemens also integrates products across units with maintenance and management services in four sectors: energy, health care, industry, and infrastructure. Siemens' service structure has transformed from simple to complex.

Configuration is the *structure* of roles, responsibilities, decision rights, resources, and rewards that is conducive to developing and delivering services and solutions. Most goods-oriented firms are organized around products or product categories, where employees attend to their own products and—in most situations—compete with other products or product categories for corporate resources and the attention of senior management and the sales force. The goods-oriented firm's managerial structure is usually hierarchical, with well-defined levels established over time.

In such organizations, managers naturally ask themselves these three tough questions:

1. Is there an optimal organizational structure for infusing services and solutions into our product or manufacturing company? If so, how much would we have to restructure?
2. How should we initially deliver these new services and solutions? Through a separate unit of the company that deals only with services, or through our existing product divisions that would deliver products, services, and solutions?
3. As we evolve our service operations, will we need to reorganize more radically away from our product orientation?

Unfortunately, there are no clear answers. Neither academic research nor executive experience points to one best way.

Furthermore, operating a new, relatively untested, and completely different division—with different personnel, policies, and structure—alongside a well-established and well-known products organization leads to conflicts over resources where the products team often wins. When firms offer services to the far right of the continuum, they need varying resources, especially people, not managed within a single unit and not easily integrated across units.

As might be expected, the five firms in our research tried many different schemes and rarely got the structure right the first time. To expedite the integration of resources, they continue to adjust their personnel, incentive, and decision-making approaches.

Where to Incubate the Service and Solution Business?

Option A: The Stand-alone Unit and Separate Resources

One study investigated 11 German capital equipment manufacturers firms in four different stages of service infusion:

1. Consolidating product-related services (i.e., entitlements);
2. Entering the installed-based service market, involving all product- or process-related services required by an end-user over the life of a product (i.e., value-added, supplementary services);
3. Offering relationship-based services (i.e., managed services, advisory services); and
4. Designing process-centered services (i.e., business process outsourcing).

Researchers concluded that a critical success factor for the transition to services is the creation of a separate services and solution organization with a dedicated sales force, information system, metrics, control system, and profit and loss status. They reasoned that traditional manufacturing organizations do not understand how to provide services and often consider them add-ons. Moreover, the revenues and profits of emerging services are small compared with the financial rewards of products. They contend that manufacturing firms must learn to value, sell, deliver, and bill service. The most successful firms in their study ran service organizations as profit centers with profit and loss responsibility, even when firms were early in their transition.[3]

We also documented the value of incubating services and solutions in the companies in our study. When they embedded services in product units, managers still emphasized products and assigned insufficient accountability for service. When one company altered its structure and placed services in a standalone business unit with its own leader, accountability, P&Ls, and decision rights, the services thrived.

Another company reorganized to place all service personnel together in one unit. Before the change, the company operated 250 different toll-free customer hotlines; after the change, it needed only one 800 number. This same company also designed a central database with customer information so that all personnel could easily access complete customer histories.

A third company began by offering services and solutions within its product strategic business units, but quickly found that these strategic business units lacked the expertise and people to sell and deliver services, although the SBUs saw services as an opportunity. When the company moved services into a separate SBU, the services and solutions SBU flourished with its own sales and delivery.

Option B: Intrafirm Collaboration and Shared Resources

In contrast to the strategy of service incubation, other studies indicate that separate service organizations will not succeed. In research involving three indepth case studies, autonomous or discrete business units created a silo mentality rather than cooperation across functional groups and business units.[4] Customers want resources and expertise from multiple units in the company, and so *intrafirm collaboration*—transferring or sharing resources to create, implement, and support the service innovation and delivery process—is essential. In intrafirm *lateral collaboration*, individuals form linkages across functional groups, business units, and geographic locations to meet their performance goals. The key measure of lateral collaboration is the *resource flows*, that is, the degree to which various business units access, acquire, or share each other's resources to support the service development process.[5] To increase resource flows, management must integrate business unit responsibilities, create incentives and reward systems for intra- and interfirm collaboration, and decentralize decision-making authority.[6] The greater the degree to which various business units in the firm share human resources, the more integrated the services and solutions can be. Separate service organizations interfere with resource flows and hinder the company's ability to deliver increasingly complex services and solutions on the right side of the continuum. DuPont, for example, has a distinct and successful service SBU. Yet, its leaders admit that the unit's autonomy limits its awareness within the larger DuPont and overlooks cross-selling opportunities from the product SBUs.[7]

What Is the Optimal Structure?

In our indepth research, firms described how their organizational structure changed as their service and solution offerings grew more complex. The optimal configuration depended on the maturity of service business within the company and the nature of the service or solution, that is, where it fell on the continuum. Companies that have successfully infused services in their portfolio created a separate service and solution division to incubate the business, either initially or after other structures failed. This autonomy protected employees from intraorganization competition for resources and empowered them to develop decision- and operating mechanisms better suited to serving their clients. Managers told us that they needed to make decisions quickly and that the product-centric hierarchy could not accommodate the speed. In the short term, they typically set up an entirely separate division to accomplish this goal. As the services and solutions matured, the business unit needed to incorporate resources from other divisions into its offerings, and so it adapted its organizational processes and structure accordingly.

A recent study corroborates our findings that the optimal structure depends on the nature of the service.[8] The researchers defined five service strategies—customer service provider, after-sales service provider, customer support service, development partner, and outsourcing partner— and then identified organizational design factors that might vary in the success of implementing these strategies. These design factors included the following:

- Culture, such as service orientation of corporate values manifested in employee behavior
- Personnel, such as recruitment, training, assessment, and compensation
- Structure, such as organizational distinctiveness between product and service businesses, and proximity to customers of the service organization.

Using cluster analysis, they developed four configurations of organizational design factors that corresponded with different strategies. They found that four of the five service categories discriminated among the four clusters, meaning that different configurations of culture, personnel, and structure corresponded with four of the five service strategies.

Consider IBM's service and solution structure over time. In 1992, IBM created a small and independent organization to manage customers' IT business processes. In 1995, the company restructured to integrate the business process outsourcing services into a new business unit called IBM Global Services, which would deliver all IBM services. In 2002, IBM acquired PricewaterhouseCoopers Consulting and restructured again into a matrix organization with 6 service lines and 18 separate industries.[9] Today, IBM's service and solution lines include (1) business strategy; (2) finance and risk; (3) information technology; (4) marketing, sales, and service; (5) operations and supply chain; and (6) organization and people. The 18 industries in which IBM has dedicated expertise are aerospace and defense, automotive, banking, chemicals and petroleum, communications, consumer products, education, electronics, energy and utilities, financial markets, government, healthcare, insurance, life sciences, media and entertainment, metals and mining, retail, and travel and transportation.

IBM and Siemens both realized that "organizational structures prevailing in goods-oriented firms are not transferable to management consulting firms."[10]

How to Integrate Services and Solutions in Stages

Firms obviously do not move service divisions from incubation to full integration rapidly, and the few published studies represent the extremes of incubation and full integration. We believe that most firms proceed through different stages as they mature and as they more fully commit to service infusion.

Flattening the Organization

Several companies in our study decentralized decision-making authority to lower levels of the firm, often by flattening the service divisions and removing multiple layers that slowed down activities. A flatter organization expedites decisions and enables employees to act more quickly on customers' needs. One company, for example, changed to a regional structure for its service and solution business, flattened decision-making for speed, and assigned local responsibility for sales and operations. The new structure eliminated silos, and sales and operations teams cooperated at the regional level to make decisions jointly, quickly, and independently of other regions. One executive told us that employee attitudes improved because senior management provided clear direction and freed them to move forward. This horizontal structure for customer-centric firms facilitates natural workflows and information sharing among team members.[11] There is also a common view of how to meet customer needs better than the competition can.[12]

Increasing Resource Flows

As the existing service business matures or as the firm offers additional services and solutions to the right on the continuum, people responsible for service design and delivery need resources from other parts of the organization. At this point, service divisions must collaborate across functions and in activities that span organizational divisions to draw on these resources. The companies in our study took several approaches to layering in such boundary-spanning roles and activities across the organization.

- One company used key account managers, segment managers, or segment task forces to coordinate customer contact activities. The more strategic the need, the more critical these roles and tasks, especially when clients were business units heads and C-suite executives.
- Another company created a service council with representatives from all the business units that sold and delivered services so that the company overall could coordinate service and solution offerings.
- A third company transferred resource management from "brand managers" or "product managers" to "customer managers" who marshaled the needed resources.

Overcoming Organizational Silos

Another means of integration is *silo busting*, the implementation of "structural mechanisms and processes that allow employees to improve their focus on the customer by harmonizing information and activities across units."[13] It is less about busting silos and more about implementing platforms that span silos and support people, although several of the firms we studied reported layering boundary-spanning roles over the current silo structure to connect the company's activities to customer needs.

Reorganizing Around Categories of Service

As one of our firms moved toward consulting, its management shifted the leadership from a regional to a practice-based structure. The firm developed four distinct practices around different competencies, each with a single leader who determined strategies, customer targets, and personnel needs rather than integrating resources of the practices. The firm supports these exclusive practices with common back-office processes that enable scaling such as capturing knowledge, marketing, sales training, and service design. General Electric with its Intelligent Services unit takes a similar approach, where there is common support for a diversity of industry expertise and applications, from health care to transportation.

Restructuring Around Front, Back and Strategic Units

When firms want to provide fully integrated product and service solutions at the far right of the continuum, they have reached the ultimate need for organizational change. Of the firms we studied, only one consistently integrated products and services for its customers; the rest provided various product–service integrations to a small number of clients. There is not enough evidence to explain why, but we suspect they need to restructure more extensively in order to design and deliver the most complex of offerings. A company could reorganize around customer accounts and customer segments for sales and marketing, but even this change requires great leadership at the top to overcome resistance from heads of product units who traditionally hold power within many product-centric firms.[14] None of the firms studied had moved to this structure.

A more comprehensive framework, the "front-back" hybrid, consists of three groupings:

- front-end customer-facing units that develop, sell, and deliver integrated solutions to customers,
- back-end product and service units that support the front-end through standardized modules of services, and
- a strategic center to mediate between the front- and back-end units.

The front-end units present a single face to customers. They specialize in customer knowledge, set revenue and profit goals for specific customer accounts or specific customer segments, and take responsibility for the growth of both top and bottom lines. They are cross-functional and have authority to assemble product, service, and solution capabilities from the entire firm and from third-party partners.

For Executive Discussion

1. What changes have you made to your organization in order to provide these services and solutions in addition to your products?
2. What configuration changes must your organization make to be successful with this service and solution?
3. What process and technology changes are needed to support the service or solution design, marketing and sales, and delivery?
4. If a separate organization is not to be established, how will the company span the boundaries between products and services and solutions?
5. Is there an optimal organizational configuration for infusing services into our product or manufacturing company? If so, how much would we have to restructure?
6. How should we initially deliver new services and solutions? Through a separate unit of the company that deals only with services, or through our existing product divisions that would deliver both products and services and solutions?
7. As we evolve our service operations, will we need to reorganize more radically away from our product orientation?
8. Where in the organization should new services and solutions be incubated?
9. Should service or solutions personnel all be placed within the same unit?
10. Is there a danger of a silo mentality if services and solutions are separated into different units?
11. Can the organization be flattened to allow the configuration to be more effective?

CHAPTER 4

Capabilities

Skills, Training, and Technology

When you hear the brand name *Sylvania*, what comes to mind? Light bulbs perhaps, or maybe television tubes? What about global consulting? Sylvania has transformed itself from a small New England light bulb recycler into the global lighting applications and services division of OSRAM AG, a leading manufacturer headquartered in Germany and part of the Siemens empire. Nearly 40 years ago, Sylvania began its service transformation by enabling its lighting design team to offer customers advice. As it developed more energy-efficient products with longer life spans and better lighting, it started helping customers to upgrade their lighting systems so that they saved energy and cut expenses. It added lighting maintenance and inspection services tailored to each customer's site and budget. More recently, Sylvania began offering an environmentally designed "ECOLOGIC" product line integrated with advisory services: Lighting specialists perform energy audits and determine the best-fit lighting system. Today, Sylvania Lighting Services spans the continuum, with 24-hour bilingual customer service, warranties, and financing programs at one end, and complete energy management and lighting system controls integration and monitoring at the other. Also, it leverages its deep expertise in lighting technology to offer not just lighting maintenance programs and energy audits but also utility rebate management, recycling, and sustainability programs.[1]

But none of this service infusion would be possible without the capabilities of key employees, particularly salespeople, service technicians, and delivery personnel. *Capabilities* are the skills and knowledge of employees who deal directly with customers and the organization's competence in developing the requisite service and solution talent, offerings, and support systems. The capabilities a company needs hinge on the services and solutions it wishes to offer along the service infusion continuum. As firms move across the continuum, they usually find themselves calling on customers with different needs higher up in the corporate hierarchy, and so the firms' capabilities must change. Our interviewees revealed that, as they moved across the continuum as Sylvania has, they had to find and develop sales and delivery personnel with the right skills and expertise. The following sections focus on the capabilities of the main customer touch points within an organization: salespeople, service technicians, service delivery personnel, and support.

Sales Capabilities

The responsibility for understanding customers' environments and value propositions to their own customers frequently falls on the sales organization. As such, salespeople need an indepth and sophisticated knowledge of their customers.[2] One of our interviewees summed up the situation, "People don't fully understand that, to be a service business, you need to know customers better than they know themselves and truly understand what makes them successful."

As a company moves across the continuum, many traditional salespeople will be ineffective in selling services and solutions for several reasons. First, services and solutions are innately more difficult to explain than products because they are less tangible. Explaining complex services and solutions is very different from explaining physical attributes of products. One interviewee said, "It's hard to demonstrate the value of services to customers. Selling the invisible or conceptual is a tougher sell, as is tying services to long-term customer value." Even more than products, services are *experienced goods*; that is, a customer must experience them before fully understanding them and appreciating their value. Customers' experience of a product is often directly transferable, whereas experience of a service and solution is not.[3]

Second, the incentive for selling some services and solutions may be considerably less than for selling products because they often have a lower price point. Lower pricing, in turn, can mean lower commissions and bonuses for the salesperson. Over time, multiyear service agreements may shrink this gap but initially it can demotivate product-oriented salespeople.

Third, through our work, we learned services and solutions at mid- to right-positions on the continuum require longer sales cycles, and the sales process is often more complex and strategic. Salespeople's customer contacts—the people who make purchase decisions about products—are often too low in the client organization's hierarchy or compartmentalized in a procurement office to sign contracts for more expensive and complex services, especially when integrated with products.[4] That is not to say that salespeople cannot learn a lot from their contacts about decision rights and organizational needs, but it requires greater investigative skills to pinpoint and connect with the key decision makers.

For example, upper-level functional managers are more likely to seek and sign up for advisory services than entry-level managers. When services and solutions address strategic problems with long-term implications for a company, the decision to hire advisors would necessarily involve the highest levels of top management. "We need to call on the C-suite because only at that level do they understand the full breadth of the value offered by our services," one senior vice president of strategy and development told us.

Furthermore, as a company moves to the right of the continuum, the sales function must transform from transactional to relationship-based selling, where clients view company representatives as trusted advisers whose customer knowledge deepens as the relationship unfolds in collaboration.[5] These representatives make unbiased recommendations about what is best for the customer, and that includes recommending competitors' products and services. A salesperson's duties resemble those of a general manager responsible for "marshaling internal and external resources to satisfy customer needs and wants."[6] The application of specialized skills and knowledge is the sales team's fundamental unit of exchange, where goods are merely distribution mechanisms for service provision.[7]

When the provider continues to learn more about the customer's business and priorities, and the customer learns more about the provider's diverse value proposition, they become partners in strategic problem solving. That is the goal. Salespeople need to understand their own company's intangible competencies, not just their physical products, and how these competencies provide value to their customers. To accomplish this transformation, the company must reward its service and solution sales representatives for aligning with other colleagues in the firm so that they can call on others' expertise to benefit the customer.[8]

Companies must also select the appropriate customer to target. Many customers may not have the long-term vision needed for a company to create successful service and solution propositions. Complex services require not only longer sales cycles but also a strong collaborative relationship between the sales team and the customer's staff.[9] An interviewee emphasized, "We have learned that it takes a willing customer—a partner—to make services work, meaning a customer who sees the 'endgame' rather than has a short-term focus."

These partnerships afford salespeople a deep level of insight into the customer. For example, these customers can provide feedback on how a service or solution will operate and affect internal customer processes and can guide the sales personnel through the customer's internal politics.[10] To facilitate the sales process, staff in charge of new business development should look for these traits in prospective customers:

- The company already has a strong relationship with the customer
- Decision makers view the service provider as a business partner
- It is evident that the company's services and solutions are likely to bring significant value to the customers
- Staff members on the client side are rewarded for collaborating with the service or solutions provider
- The customer has an adequate level of knowledge to assess the value of the solution and understand how the solution affects their internal processes.
- The existence of cross-unit relationship ties between the provider and customer organization such as relationships across numerous business units or functional roles.

Moving across the continuum often mandates a more senior sophisticated account manager who can focus engagement discussions on customer outcomes linked to the proposed services or solutions.[11] Furthermore, the complexity and magnitude of the services or solutions proposed frequently call for multiple ties at multiple levels throughout the customers' business units frequently.[12] One of our interviewees said, "The capabilities of sales-people are the biggest limitation for our growth. Most are unable to do consultative selling and offer customers outcome-oriented proposals that address [the customer's key performance indicators]."

Companies must also develop professional consultative selling capa-bilities. Salespeople who take a consultative approach tend to perform at higher levels than their counterparts with a technical specialist iden-tity.[13] Sometimes the firm's human resources staff will need to recruit high-level account managers from industries that the firm is targeting; that means that HR must develop a wider recruiting network beyond the firm's current industry sector. Many of our participating companies do this and provide ongoing training on key customer segments and industry concerns. Firms can also structure account teams around customer rela-tionship owners (i.e., account executives) supported by industry experts and technical specialists.[14] Finally, this professional selling requires acute listening skills, interpersonal adeptness, collaboration, and the ability to think on one's feet. One interviewee noted, "Sales people need to be 'quar-terbacks' for the customer, combining different services" just as quarter-backs on football teams call different plays according to the situation.

This transition in sales is difficult for many salespeople.[15] "50 percent of sales people cannot be successful selling services—some are unwilling, others are incapable," said one interviewee. If a firm cannot retrain these people, then it can replace them or restrict them to selling services that support products. A firm can also offer quality training, coaching, and special incentives to those interested and capable of selling higher-level service offerings.

Service and Solution Delivery Capabilities

The sales, service delivery, and marketing functions need stronger connec-tions that result in collaboration and alignment among these groups to face the customer in an integrated way.[16]

To deliver services and solutions on the mid and right portions of the continuum, companies require people who possess both business and technical acumen, not just technicians. Service delivery personnel must act entrepreneurially with both the big picture and the long term in mind. Hiring managers should look beyond job candidates' technical expertise to their interpersonal skills and behavioral competencies that fortify relationships and customer-focused attitudes.[17] People in service delivery positions must be able to listen carefully, learn quickly, respond quickly, anticipate customers' needs, and engender support across their own firm. These attributes contribute to greater customer satisfaction and loyalty—two key metrics of success—and so firms should reward their delivery staff accordingly. Leading firms are also recruiting and retaining people with technical knowledge and then subsequently training them on the customer-focused necessities of service and solution delivery.

Finally, companies must reposition service as a desirable career path in a product-oriented company. Attracting top people outside and internally for service and solution opportunities is still a challenge. "Many employees are reluctant to join the services unit, because it doesn't 'fit' in their minds. Further, there is not a career growth path for individuals in the services unit as there is for individuals in other divisions," said one of the executives in our study.

Other Customer-Centric Capabilities

The companies we studied all recognize that service infusion requires not just more associates, but more associates with the right talents and skills. For example, larger and longer service and solution engagements often require project managers who oversee the completion of projects on time, on budget, and to customer-defined standards.[18]

To escalate service and solution growth, companies must also enhance systems and technology. Interviewees specifically discussed the need to incorporate key technology platforms to get closer to their customer. For example, knowledge management systems enable staff to capture, codify, and share companywide what they have learned while selling and servicing clients. When mined properly, these systems can alert companies to faulty service design and can guide service upgrades and innovation. The firms we studied also sought to "webify" services where possible, that is, to automate services through online help menus, project dashboards, expert wikis, and other diagnostic tools, yet enable clients to access live talent through call centers or online chats. Customer relationship management (CRM) systems help to scale services and solutions without sacrificing customer intimacy. One company in our study implemented an interactive voice response (IVR) system that routes customer calls to informational audio tracks or to a live representative depending on their menu selections. Other companies, such as Time Warner Cable, are experimenting with IVR systems that can reboot client systems remotely. If the problem is too sophisticated for IVR, then clients can reach live representatives and, if necessary, schedule an on-site appointment with a technician. By studying clients' menu choices and recording conversations, the provider can learn more about the customer's trouble spots and the service staff's training needs. Moreover, recorded calls can surface the language the customers most often use in describing problems, and the marketing department can leverage this language on the website and in search-driven campaigns.

Simply assigning existing people the task of growing higher-end services and solutions will likely fail. Instead, company leaders must assess who, among current sales and service delivery associates, has the ambition and the talent to grow into the more complex roles required of service infusion. Then the organization must make a significant commitment to training, motivating, and coaching these employees. Concurrently, most firms will likely need to recruit some high-level account executives skilled in problem solving, collaborating, and interacting with high-level executives within the customers' organizations. Finally, corporate marketing must build awareness of their organization's new services and solutions. That involves promotions to a higher-level audience, including testimonials from clients, participation of corporate experts in vertical conferences, and research and publication of service and solution outcomes in white papers and trade and scholarly journal articles.

For Executive Discussion

As you reflect upon the sales and delivery functions and other customer touch points within your organization, here are some prompts to guide your exploration and conversations. The point is to determine the capabilities that you have and those that you need. Again, put these questions to your management team and compare your understanding of the sales, delivery, and support functions.

Sales Capabilities

1. Have we re-conceptualized the sales role, its responsibilities, and its rewards, paying salespeople for aligning with other colleagues in the firm so that they can draw on others' expertise when designing value propositions?

2. Do our salespeople have an indepth and sophisticated knowledge of our customers?

3. Do they excel at articulating the benefits of our services and solutions and explaining how we develop, deliver, and support these offerings? Can they link our services and solutions to short, intermediate, and long-term customer value?

4. Are incentives for service and solution sales commensurate with or even disproportionate to product sales? Have we set goals with longer sales cycles or are we simply replicating what we have done in the product units?

5. Have we helped the sales staff to understand the payoff associated with multiyear service agreements?

6. For services and solutions that address very strategic problems with long-term implications for a company, do we have access to C-suite decision makers?

7. How have we designed the sales function for services and solutions? Is it more transactional or more relationship based?

8. How well do our salespeople understand our company's intangible competencies, not just our physical products, and how these competencies provide value to their customers?

9. Are our sales representatives prepared to integrate our competitors' offerings into our own?

10. For higher value service and solutions offerings, should the salesperson's or account executive's duties resemble those of a general manager responsible for marshaling internal and external resources to satisfy customer needs?

11. To what extent is our sales team's view service-centered, customer oriented, and relational rather than product centric, SBU oriented, and transactional?

12. What is the fundamental unit of exchange? Is it the application of specialized skills and knowledge to customers' problems? Are goods merely distribution mechanisms for service provision? Or is it the application of a component or a product?

13. Have we identified customers higher up in client organizations who have a long-term vision and a willingness to collaborate? Do the decision makers view us as a business partner? Does the client reward staff members for collaborating with us?

14. Do we need more sophisticated senior account managers and account executives who can focus engagement discussions on customer outcomes linked to existing and proposed services and solutions? Can they do consultative selling and create customers outcome-oriented proposals that address the customer's key performance indicators? Do they exhibit acute listening skills, interpersonal adeptness, collaborative effort, and the ability to think on their feet?

15. Do we provide ongoing training on key customer segments and industry concerns so that sales representatives and account managers can spot opportunities?

16. Have we structured account teams around customer relationship owners (i.e., account executives) and supported them with industry experts and technical specialists? Why or why not?

17. Are we offering quality training, coaching, and special incentives to those sales staff who are capable of selling higher-level service or solution offerings?

Service Delivery Capabilities

1. Do our service and solution delivery people possess both business and technical acumen, or are they primarily technicians?

2. Do they act entrepreneurially?

3. Do they grasp both the big picture and the long-term goals of the customer beyond tactical and technical concerns?

4. Do delivery associates demonstrate the ability to pamper customers and develop personal relationships?

5. Are our hiring managers looking beyond each job candidates' technical expertise? Are they deliberately engaging each candidate's interpersonal skills and other behavioral competencies that fortify relationships?

6. Do our people in service and solution delivery positions listen carefully, learn quickly, respond quickly, anticipate customers' needs, and engender support across their own firm? What metrics and feedback mechanisms can we use to assess these capabilities? Perhaps customer satisfaction and loyalty?

7. Have we repositioned service as a desirable career path in our company? Are we attracting top people outside and internally for service and solution opportunities? Why are employees reluctant to join the services or solutions unit?

Other Customer-Centric Capabilities

1. Does HR need to recruit high-level account managers, account executives, or other talent from industries that we are targeting? Is HR staff willing and able to cultivate a wider recruiting network beyond our current industry sector?

2. Do we need project managers for larger and longer service or solution engagements? Are we capable of recruiting or developing necessary project management skills?

3. Should we enhance systems and technology to support and improve the sale and delivery of services and solutions? What technology platforms might we incorporate to serve customers better? Knowledge management systems? Automated customer service or IVR systems? CRM systems?

4. Is our marketing team able to capture and communicate the intangible competencies of existing and new services and solutions in promotional copy and in other ways?

5. Has our marketing team accurately assessed and impartially compared the benefits and drawbacks of our competitors' products, services, and solutions side by side with our own?

6. Is marketing building awareness of our services and solutions? Are they reaching out and connecting with a higher-level audience? Are they soliciting and leveraging testimonials from clients?

7. How can we capture, codify, and promote our organization's knowledge and expertise in services and solutions? Are our knowledgeable people participating in vertical conferences, conducting research in their area of expertise within the company, and publishing outcomes in white papers and trade and scholarly journal articles?

CHAPTER 5

Customization

Balancing Uniqueness with Operational Realities

In the publishing industry, Pearson PLC dominates the world's education market. Its teaching and learning materials touch all grades and settings, from preschool to postdoctorate and from home schooling to the corporate university.

For the last 15 years, Pearson has been acquiring educational technology firms and online training outfits in anticipation of digital reading and the emergence of a global middle-class consumer. According to *The Times* of London, "Every year over the next decade one hundred million people in emerging markets such as China, India, and Brazil will join the middle classes. Every year they will spend $1 trillion more on goods and services such as education."[1] Pearson wants a major chunk of that discretionary spending. It now owns the major vocational training ventures in India, and its English language training programs in China are growing at double-digit rates.[2]

To that end, Pearson is merging its Penguin trade book division with Random House, owned by Bertlesmann AG. This divestiture frees its operations to focus on academic services. "The bigger picture," says Ian King of *The Times*, "is that…Pearson has been reshaped along the lines of a fast-moving consumer goods business, like Unilever, to better target growth markets and to aid the move from print to digital."[3] But, unlike consumer goods marketers, Pearson's progress up the service infusion continuum has positioned it to capitalize on the decrease in public funding for education: instead of depending on government bulk purchases of print inventory, Pearson is increasingly providing school systems with administrative services and online training solutions that better suit country, state, and local budgets and individual school needs.

In 2012, Pearson's sales were up five percent at a constant exchange rate to £6.1 billion, with digital and services businesses comprising half of those sales. Not bad, considering two of its major U.S. competitors—Houghton Mifflin Harcourt, Cengage Learning, and School Specialty, Inc.—declared (or emerged from) bankruptcy during the same period.

The Drive to Customize

What made Pearson's growth possible? Its ability to customize. Pearson's portfolio includes not just textbooks and ancillary packages—instructor's manuals, test banks, presentation packages, study guides, and workbooks—but also copyrighted software and patented delivery platforms. Pearson digitized all its content to industry standards so that it could (1) mix and match chunks of material according to each customer's curriculum requirements and even to individual student's learning deficits, and then (2) plug this material into its course management or assessment platforms, installed on the customer's servers or hosted in the cloud. In other words, Pearson can create customized solutions from a standardized set of digital goods and services.

Customization involves tailoring offerings to customers' needs. As companies such as Pearson move from the left of the continuum—where, for example, Pearson was shipping textbooks and ancillaries in bulk—to the right side, where Pearson now provides classroom administrative tools, online learning management systems, and both student and teacher testing services, customers begin expecting greater customization on four dimensions:[4]

1. The service or solution offering must meet the customer's unique requirements fully, including accommodating its internal processes and being consistent with its business model.
2. The offering must fit into the customer's culture and operating environment.
3. The provider must not only design but also deploy the customized offering, including installing, modifying, and maintaining the solution and addressing any issues that arise.

4. After deployment, the provider must keep up with—and even ahead of—the customer's evolving requirements.

One cannot help viewing customization as an ongoing relationship between supplier and customer.[5] The actual tailoring of the service or solution often comes largely from face-to-face interactions with clients, not in the back office of corporate headquarters. That said, manufacturers must design new services and solutions, as well as delivery processes and performance standards, as sharply as they engineer new products and production processes. And so, when lead customers request a new higher-end service or solution, the supplier should consider developing a pilot to model the offering and learn from the implementation. If the pilot works for both the client and the supplier, then the supplier can decide whether to replicate or adapt the offering for other customers. The benefits are clear: the supplier is more likely to discover viable new offerings and the customer is less likely to switch because the costs of finding, vetting, and implementing a comparable offering would be high. Companies such as IBM, GE, Avnet, and DuPont often use this "first-of-a-kind" or piloting approach for higher-end new services and solutions.

Advisory services are often highly customized because the provider must deeply understand the client's situation—its environment, history, and people—which varies across clients even within an industry, and therefore necessitates different advice. Even if situations are common—for example, all publishers are grappling with the Internet and mobile technology—suppliers may agree to exclusivity, that is, not serving a client's competitors or not sharing what they learn from others in the same industry.

Managed services are also often customized because the offering may span multiple sites and countries. For example, Hewlett-Packard and Xerox both developed management services that helped large companies replace desktop printers and copiers with shared multifunctional devices and transfer files to digital storage rather than physical archives. These devices and virtual archiving vastly reduced the number of machines at Dow Chemical, cut printing costs by 20 to 30 percent, and facilitated conservation of resources, efficiencies in servicing and maintenance, better accountability of printing costs, and savings in space, maintenance, and electricity.[6] The conditions of these managed services varied greatly across clients. While virtually all contracts involved monthly fees, some required exclusivity, and others deployed only the supplier's own printers.

For large, profitable, and reputable customers (and prospects) who can fund the company's growth, a company might offer high levels of customization. However, customization of *all* offers for *all* clients—at all positions along the continuum—is costly, often unnecessary, and usually undesirable. Suppliers may believe that service and solution customization is easier and cheaper than with products, but it is not: Customization can incur high opportunity costs. Responding uniquely to every customer request can create complexity without necessarily better serving customer needs; it may, in fact, lead to a complexity of choice, inconsistency, and unmet promises. "Too much emphasis on customization can impede the provision of repeatable solutions...but the pendulum cannot swing too far the other way: There are limits to standardization and replication."[7]

The key is to determine how much to standardize to gain efficiencies and provide consistency in service delivery and how much to customize.

What to Standardize?

All the executives in our study spoke of standardizing elements of service, even complex high-end service activities at the far right of the continuum. This standardization benefits the company by reducing costs, setting expectations, and increasing customer satisfaction.

First, firms that develop and deploy process maps and templates enable their employees to deliver services—particularly those in high demand—consistently and efficiently to all customers. Second, standardization clarifies roles and responsibilities for salespeople and support staff so that they can articulate what they are selling and how they will deliver it to customers. Third, standardization facilitates performance measurement so that firms can identify best practices and areas for improvement. Our companies emphasized the need to codify content and methodologies across the organization and to standardize the training offered to contact personnel. Too much standardization, on the other hand, can lead to commoditization and lack of differentiation.

Harvard Business School professor Theodore Levitt suggested that companies first inventory all the service activities that employees perform, and then either systematize those done uniquely each time or plan those done ad hoc.[8] He favored re-engineering these activities in three ways:

- Replace human activities with technology-based processes or what he called *hard technologies*;
- Bundle human activities into processes, packages, or modules, which Leavitt referred to as *soft technologies*; and
- Combine the hard and the soft into *hybrid technologies*.

In theory, a company can integrate any or all of these standardized components seamlessly into a large set of unique offerings, with costs, performance benchmarks, and accountability attached to each element and assignable overall. In practice, neither employees nor customers can manage such variety, complexity, and cost. Therefore, companies standardize and customize on a more limited basis as described in the following section.

How to Standardize?

Both customization and standardization have benefits, and companies need to customize without losing the efficiency, and standardize without losing the customer-centric differentiation.

Create Service Modules

Our respondents talked about mass customization or creating modular units that sales associates can assort and match in unique combinations for each customer. If modules are consistent, easy to understand, and easy to assemble—much like Lego bricks—then contact personnel can simply select what the client needs from an existing portfolio of modules rather than developing all new services for every new project or client. This modular approach cuts costs and improves the reliability of the integrated services and solutions. The supplier can revise these service modules as needed to improve the process of selling and delivering solutions.

In addition to menus of modules, our interviewees used service blueprint-ing, process mapping, value maps, templates, and lean six sigma to stan-dardize elements, describe value, and continually improve their offerings.

Use Centers of Excellence

To ensure quality and consistency of employees' delivery of service, our firms have taken several approaches. One company created a center of excellence that focused on documenting best practices and delivery pro-cesses, then implementing these consistently throughout the company. Another developed standard e-learning modules to replicate delivery and knowledge across the firm. Another found that outside firms with consult-ing experience could serve as centers of excellence if they had developed mechanisms for training associates to perform consistently. The supplier could simply hire them and learn their techniques. Another mapped out processes and developed templates and tools to ensure a level of consis-tency for sales managers.

Train Customer-Facing Staff

Some companies trained sales staff to address such customer-facing activities as defining the problem and proposing a solution. Training includes listening skills to assess customer needs and to understand their issues, industry, and company. They learn how to match standardized modules of back-office capabilities to address these needs. Said one of our most advanced interviewees, "70 to 80 percent of solutions are based on standardized modules." Advisory services comprised the remaining 20 to 30 percent.

Prepare Back-Office Staff

Standardized modules help not only the personnel who sell the services and solutions but also the staff who actually perform them in such areas as product development, marketing, communications, human resources, professional services, and systems integrations. Ericsson reports that it bases up to 75 percent of the service component of its integrated solutions on its off-the-shelf reusable modules. The modular approach cuts costs and improves the reliability of the integrated solutions—but only if everyone involved in implementation understands their role in achieving performance objectives and can flag potential problems with new configurations.[9]

Identify Economies of Scale

Companies can standardize those services that "call for high volumes, low variable costs, and the high utilization of fixed assets"—such as common business processes or monitoring services that depend on networks and sensor technology—to achieve economies of scale.[10] For example, automated transaction processing scales almost infinitely when standardized, thereby helping companies such as Automatic Data Processing to realize low unit costs and high margins. Businesses that can scale their services also benefit from positive network effects—that is, the more they do, the more they can do—and so they depend on globally dispersed assets, such as distribution centers (for supply chain services), data centers (for IT outsourcers), or payment platforms and protocols (for procurement and payroll providers).[11]

Limit the Complexity of Service Offerings

Services businesses must clarify decision rights that limit customized requests to what is doable, profitable, or strategically advantageous, and consistent with the corporate brand and mission. "Sales and service personnel often agree to address customized requests, but across an organization they can add up to a major productivity drain."[12] With the exception of highly profitable advisory services and solutions, companies should offer clients a limited service menu that includes the most common requests and then train or otherwise incentivize service personnel to refrain from performing or offering to perform extra work that falls outside the billable model.[13] Companies can also build service cost models to determine which of the many requests that are requested by clients are worthwhile to create.

Limit the Set of Technology Platforms

In one project, the extent of technological variation among the different services "manifested in problems concerning service quality and increased production costs."[14] The company created a limited set of offering platforms to deliver the targeted functionalities, instead of deploying 10 separate offerings to provide the same functionalities. The engineers based the targeted offering platforms on a handful of selected software technologies, and that decision further reduced the software complexity. They then divided them into core functionalities and peripheral functionalities.

For Executive Discussion

Are We Ready for Customization?

1. Are we already customizing products, services, and solutions for customers? Where, how, and why?
2. How do we respond to customers' requests for:
   - Services and solutions that meet their unique requirements fully, including their internal processes and business models?
   - Services and solutions that fit into their culture and operating environment?
   - Services and solutions that we not only design but also install, modify, and maintain?
   - Upgrades to meet customers' evolving requirements?
3. Where do we have strong relationships with customers?
   - What can we learn from our customer-facing personnel about customers' emergent needs? Any patterns?
   - How can we involve our lead customers in exploring potential new higher-end services and solutions and in experimenting with pilot programs?
   - Which customers will likely welcome experimentation?
4. What have we learned in engineering new products and production processes that we can apply in designing new services or solutions, delivery processes, and performance standards?

- What is the value of exclusivity—that is, providing a particular customized solution for only one company within a market or an industry—to service R&D? What can we learn, that we can provide to clients in other markets or industries?
- What is the value of incorporating and servicing only our products into a customized solution?
- How can we cost out customer service and solution requests? Can we build service cost models?
- How can we sort the weak signals of emerging needs from the costly customization?

What Can We Standardize?

1. Which service activities are we already performing? Take a thorough inventory.
2. Which activities do customers expect employees to perform, but employees are doing them uniquely each time? Can we create scripts or process maps to standardize performance?
3. Which activities are unexpected, and so employees are doing them ad hoc? Can we plan for these activities?
4. Of these activities, which can we
   - Automate or outsource services to customers by using smart technologies, technology-based processes, and customer interfaces?
   - Bundle into processes, packages, or modules for employees to do consistently?
   - Integrate the use of technology into what our employees do?
5. Where can we achieve economies of scale? Which service activities have high demand, low variable costs, and high utilization of fixed assets?

How Should We Standardize?

1. Can we create *service modules*? How can we use process maps, value maps, templates, and lean six sigma to standardize elements, describe value, and continually improve offerings?

2. Can we create *centers of excellence* or leverage outside expertise? Where does knowledge and expertise reside within our company or our value chain?

   • Are we documenting best practices and delivery processes, and then implementing these consistently throughout the company?

   • Are we learning all that we can from our supply chain partners or other industry experts?

3. Can we implement *training programs* for

   • Customer-facing staff so that they can assess customer needs, understand their issues, industry, and company, and translate this understanding into viable services and solutions?

   • Back-office staff so that they can achieve performance objectives and flag potential problems with new configurations?

4. Can we standardize *environments and tasks* by introducing standard tool kits, similar workstations, and scripts for service calls?

5. Can we introduce *conceptual frameworks* for problem-solving and scheduling charts for delineating time frames and checkpoints?

6. How can we manage complexity?

   • Can we limit customization to what is doable, profitable, and strategically advantageous, and consistent with our corporate brand and mission?

   • Who should be involved in the decision making for more complex requests? Who has decision rights?

   • Can we create a small number of delivery platforms? How can we limit the diversity of technology required and yet deliver the desired functionalities?

CHAPTER 6

Collaboration with Customers

Engaging Customers in Service and Solution Design, Development, and Delivery

VWR International is the world's second largest laboratory supply and distribution company. It supplies its scientific laboratory customers with over 8,000 different items. VWR had become an expert in the myriad of activities associated with running a laboratory, but it struggled to differentiate itself from its competitors. After working closely with customers to design a robust set of services, VWR's leaders realized that the company could capitalize on its customers' interest in science and expertise in scientific research, facilities management, and operations. The company launched a new brand, "VWR Catalyst," to collaborate with customers in reducing operating costs, increasing laboratory productivity, and adding value to the scientific process. In recent years, Catalyst has posted significant double-digit growth. You might call it a model "collaboratory."

Software company Salesforce.com sees collaboration as a key to its future. Most of its major clients consider this fast-growing enterprise a business partner, but not a trusted adviser. By collaborating with its clients, Salesforce.com can discover how better to leverage its core competencies, develop its industry thought leadership in sales, and act in each client's best longer-term interest, thereby establishing a reputation for trusted advisory services.

This chapter examines how companies such as VWR and Sales-force.com can collaborate more effectively with customers across the service continuum. We define *customer collaboration* as the involvement of customers in the process of generating ideas, designing, developing, producing, and delivering service and solution offerings. Our definition encompasses the process end to end, from idea generation, service improvement, and service or solution design through service delivery, service usage, troubleshooting, and feedback. This broad view of collaboration lines up with current, customer-defined views of service solutions[1] and research on engaging customers in new service development.[2] It also builds upon both traditional and contemporary views of new product development and service innovation.[3]

One of the fundamental premises and unique aspects of service management is that, in service production and consumption, the provider and the customer are often already collaborating to some degree.[4] In some cases, customers co-produce services and realize their benefits simultaneously by enacting their relatively prescribed role, as in routine training or consulting sessions. In other cases, customers realize the true value of the service over time.[5] For example, customers who signed up for Michelin's "pay for kilometers" tire fleet solution or GE Healthcare's imaging machine solutions experience the value of the service throughout its lifecycle; they pay for and co-create value with the provider when they use the products and equipment. In still other cases, service companies provide the facilities, the materials, and the guidance for the customers themselves to produce and deliver the needed solutions. At the extreme, this customer collaboration is a form of B2B self-service.[6] Through their involvement, customers influence service productivity, service quality, and their own satisfaction, sometimes in unpredictable ways.[7]

The key questions are to what extent do we involve customers, in which stages of the process do we involve customers, which customers do we involve, and how do we manage expectations? According to several interviewees, the key to success across the board is managing customer expectations, from carefully defining and agreeing upon the scope of work and communicating any changes in scope throughout, so as not to disappoint or surprise customers at the end of the process or project.

How Much to Collaborate?
From Surveys to Self-Service

All the executives in our study saw the value of gathering customer feedback. They described how they collaborate with customers across the continuum, starting with basic customer satisfaction surveys, focus groups, and interviews. The strongest evidence of customer participation in co-design and co-development falls at the far right end of the continuum, in integrated product–service solutions, where providers must work closely with clients to customize for particular contexts.

Our participating companies distilled what they learned to improve existing services, deploy existing services in new contexts, or to uncover ideas for new offerings.

Improvement or Speciation of Existing Services

All the companies in our study used variations of these basic types of customer participation, although some engaged in the activities more than others. One industrial firm executive reported, "We also do forums where we bring in 200 customers for a three-day meeting in which we share everything with them—challenges, technical problems, and so forth. This is beneficial because customers appreciate it but also because customers often become part of the solution." During such sessions, companies learn not only how and where to improve their services for existing clients and contexts but also how they can adapt these services and solutions for new environments. For example, companies that offer sensor-driven monitoring services to ensure building security can look to apply sensor technology for improving building energy usage.

Development of New Services and Solutions

To identify and understand customers' points of pain that new services and solutions might alleviate, companies deploy their sales representatives to interview customers one-on-one. Beyond that, companies set up client advisory boards, hold user conferences, conduct end-of-project reviews, and call on customers to test prototypes.

Research shows that companies are generating new value with their customers not simply by gathering ideas or testing prototypes but also by designing the offering and developing the customer experience.[8] The benefits of such involvement are more new services and solutions that better suit customer needs, generate greater satisfaction, and strengthen customer loyalty and firm profitability. Plus, fewer new offerings fail when customers are involved early on.[9] Moreover, the sales process parallels if not melds with the service or solution development process, such that the sales representatives and the customers involved understand the resulting offering better: the representatives know how to sell it and can contribute to sales training, and the customers can use it immediately and even advocate for wider adoption within their organizations or supply chain.

A word of caution: one B2B product innovation study across 143 customer–manufacturer dyads in different industries indicates that two different forms of customer participation—information resource and co-developer—in the early stages of product innovation participation can help or hinder innovativeness and speed to market depending on specific circumstances in the market. For example, if a new service incorporates disruptive technology, then customers may not be able to imagine an equally disruptive application.

There is much room here for companies to distinguish themselves by involving customers throughout the new service or solution development process, because even the most creative of the above approaches deals only with the beginning stages of new offerings. Despite the evidence from product and business-to-consumer service research and theoretical publications that promote customer collaboration in service design and development, our study found relatively little evidence of deep customer involvement in design or development of B2B service or solution offerings.[10]

Matching the Right Customers with the Right Capabilities

Despite a strong belief in the value of gathering customer input, our interviewees were unsure how to identify the right customers to involve, how to dedicate the needed time and resources for customer collaboration, and how to develop collaboration competencies in sales and other frontline professionals in asking and listening appropriately.

"Customers co-create 'first of a kind' offerings with us," one of our interviewees said. "Then, we try to take this intellectual capital to other customers." Several companies co-designed and field tested an initial offering of a particular service with a partner prior to launching more widely. In some cases, these "first of a kind" offerings proved "one of a kind" services that they could not easily replicate. Clearly, there may be limitations or downsides to engaging customers in service innovation.[11] The greater a testing environment represents a majority of customers, the more replicable the service will be. The extent to which the company involves the customer in testing a prototype offering, the greater that customer should eventually be involved in the new offering; a successful design, creation, and test of a complex service with a sophisticated customer may yield a service initially for similarly sophisticated customers. Advisory services can bring less sophisticated customers up to speed so they can play a role in delivery and usage.

Finding the right customers to involve in this type of concept and prototype testing effort can be challenging. As one firm's executive put it, "Sometimes we're engaging the wrong customers for tests and pilots. For various reasons, these customers weren't clear that they were part of a test and they are disappointed when the service isn't actually offered or fully implemented in the end."

In designing solutions, research shows that collaboration deepens a company's understanding of its customers' collective and relational goals.[12] In another consumer service context, a strong customer orientation and the ability to collaborate with stakeholders—employees, partners, and customers—drives service innovativeness, and this ingenuity positively affects firm performance.[13] Beyond design and development of service offerings, collaboration with customers in real-time service delivery and co-creation activities both during and after the sale can define success and build stronger relationships.[14]

There may be an optimal level of sales force customer orientation.[15] One study showed that most firms today look for customer-oriented employees and encourage their sales people to listen for opportunities to customize product or service offerings, but they need not. Ideally, the sales representative's level of customer orientation should increase as the service's or solution's importance to the customer increases. In other words, the more customized or higher priced the offering, or the more competitive the marketplace, the more customer oriented the sales representatives.[16] These conditions characterize many services and solutions on the right side of the continuum, but not those on the left side, where companies can deploy a less customer-focused sales force and involve customers minimally.

Managing the Expectations of Collaborators

When we asked whether the companies collaborated more deeply with customers in offering services and solutions on the right side of the continuum—particularly whether they did more than talk to customers prior to developing services—companies expressed concerns about deeper involvement. They told us that they strive to align customer expectations at the beginning of the project with outcomes at the end, but maintaining alignment is difficult for a number of reasons. First, the ultimate service offering may look very different from what the customer tested or initially discussed. Second, the customer feedback and test results may lead the company not to offer the service. An executive from an industrial firm told us, "In the end, you risk alienating those whose ideas you don't use, so this requires time and hand-holding to explain to them and help them understand why you didn't use their ideas or why you killed the project notwithstanding their enthusiasm."

Companies can involve sales staff in monitoring and managing expectations. For example, in the development of new course content for the college level, academic publishers such as Pearson regularly ask their sales force to identify professors who would be willing and qualified to participate in the process. Project managers provide sales representatives with a list of qualifications and a description of the process. Sales training covers how to qualify customers to participate in improvement and new offering development and how to manage customer expectations throughout.

New higher education offerings generally require a mix of (1) seasoned professors who have taught the course for years, use the market leading textbook, and can articulate what works, what does not, and why in the new material, (2) new professors who rely heavily on the supplementary materials such as the instructor's manual and test bank, (3) professors who control large purchase decisions at key schools, and (4) excellent teachers who can author or vet the supplements, test bank items, and other elements of the learning system. The level of engagement is staged: some professors complete surveys of their current textbooks; others carefully review and provide written feedback on the new content chapter by chapter; still others participate in focus groups to discuss their unmet needs; and, lastly, a few professors test the prototype in one of their class sections and gather student feedback on each chapter. Sales representatives check in with the professors throughout the process and submit additional feedback to the project manager, marketing manager, and sales management. Each element goes through user experience testing, quality assurance, and final review for accuracy, consistency, and interoperability of the whole package.

For Executive Discussion

Across our continuum from entitlement services through integrated solutions, the literature suggests that both providers and customers benefit from strategically collaborating in co-creation and co-delivery, from idea generation, to purchase, to use. The degree of collaboration should increase as firms offer services and solutions further to the right on the continuum.

In GE's quest to design and develop advanced services and solutions built on intelligent machines, software, and analytics, it typically seeks out one or a small number of existing customers to initially collaborate with. For example, before more widely introducing a new service, GE Transportation's Software and Optimization Software unit initially worked intimately with Norfolk Southern Railroad to help it optimize hundreds of rail schedules and train speeds. Norfolk estimates that an increase of just one mile per hour in its locomotives' speeds will save it over $200 million annually.

Despite, this example and a few others we have found, for the most part, when asked about customer collaboration, none of our interviewees discussed co-production or co-delivery of value.

Engaging Customers in Service and Solution Design and Delivery

1. Where do we already involve customers in the process of generating ideas, designing, developing, producing, and delivering service or solution offerings and gathering feedback on usage?
   - To what extent do we involve customers?
   - In which stages of the process do we involve customers?
   - Which customers do we involve?
   - How do we manage expectations?
2. How do we gather customer feedback?
   - Customer satisfaction surveys
   - Focus groups
   - User forums or conferences
   - End-of-project reviews
   - Client advisory boards
   - Prototype testing
   - One-on-one interviews
   - Other_____
3. Who gathers and uses this feedback?
   - Sales representatives
   - Product or project managers
   - Marketing team
   - Other_____
4. What do we do with customer feedback?
   - Improve existing services and solutions
   - Adapt offerings for new environments.
   - Develop new services and solutions
   - Other_____
5. Where do we fall short?
   - In meeting or exceeding customer needs?
   - In generating greater satisfaction?
   - In strengthening customer loyalty?
   - In increasing firm profitability?
   - In success rate of new launches?
   - In other areas_____?
6. How might we collaborate with customers to improve in these areas?

7. How can we distinguish ourselves from the competition by involving our customers more?

Matching Customers and Capabilities

1. Can we identify the right customers to involve?
2. Can we dedicate the time and resources needed to manage customer collaboration?
3. Should we enhance collaboration competencies in sales and other frontline professionals?
4. Which kind of new services and solutions have we co-created with customers?
   - "First of a kind' offerings that we can extend to other customers
   - "One of a kind" services and solutions that we cannot easily replicate.
   - Some combination of the two
5. What is the optimal level of sales force customer orientation?
   - Is our service or solution especially important to customers?
   - Is our service or solution highly customized or higher priced than other offerings?
   - Is our marketplace highly competitive?

If we answered yes to the above, then we probably need more customer-oriented sales representatives.

Managing expectations

1. Have we defined the role we want customers to play?
2. How do we train customers for this role?
3. How do we keep them informed of process?
4. How do we communicate decisions and rationales?
5. Have we appropriately recognized their contributions to the process?
6. How can we involve sales staff in selecting customers to participate?
7. How can we involve and reward sales staff in monitoring and managing expectations?

CHAPTER 7

Challenges to Offering New Services and Solutions

"We used to do monitoring and diagnostics," said Mark Little, the director of global research at GE. He was referring to GE's use of sensor technology on gas turbines, where GE would alert customers to blips in the functioning of these engines and explain how to fix them. GE is now upgrading its service offerings dramatically by leveraging "the Industrial Internet," commonly known as "the Internet of Things," where every physical object has a digital representative. Combining powerful predictive software with the sensors embedded in GE's products and networked to report on operations, and you get unprecedented prognostic capabilities. GE's new services and solutions are able not only to optimize performance and energy usage of engines in trains, airplanes, and power plants but also to anticipate trouble and eliminate unplanned downtime. Such services and solutions will help clients to maximize value and minimize risk.[1]

As firms move from left to right on the continuum, challenges change and typically increase, but so does the technology and talent needed to address them. GE has embraced these changes so that it can innovate in products, services, and solutions, often simultaneously. For example, GE's engineers use three-dimensional, computer-aided design software to model jet components on a computer screen. Where they once had to call on the tool and die guys to manufacture a prototype, they can now apply nanotechnology: They send their design file to a 3D laser printer, and the laser constructs the part in three dimensions using fine metal powder. GE can test the new part several times that very day.[2] If GE wanted to, it could build a service or solutions business around this technology, creating prototypes for smaller product design firms, training its clients' engineers on the use of the software, or renting out the printing stations to those who cannot afford their own machines.

Our firms discussed many different challenges, but the most prominent ones are those that GE is proving adept at facing: (1) investing strategically for growth in services and solutions; (2) creating metrics appropriate for services; (3) developing value propositions and pricing; and (4) working with partners.

Investing Strategically for Service and Solution Growth

Probably the most compelling strategic challenge for several of our firms involved time to market, a quandary because senior management viewed the issue completely differently from those developing higher-level services and solutions. Senior managers typically want to know how quickly the offerings will get to market, what the return on investment will be, and how quickly the firm will realize that return. Developers of services and solutions cannot answer those questions meaningfully without knowing whether they will have the resources to hire new personnel, collaborate with customers or other stakeholders in the development and delivery, and train staff in selling the service or solution, delivering per specifications, and following up on usage. One of our respondents stated, "It takes time to get the resource commitment for services. Early on we had resourcing challenges because our internal budgeting process is set for products; there wasn't a clear understanding of the need for people and investment in people that drives a consulting practice in the company."

Similarly, management generally understands that services and solutions can generate growth and high returns, but when it comes to investing in people to realize that growth, managers see little need. In general, our firms reported that executives from goods-oriented firms talk the language of capital investments and financial return easily for products, but not for services and solutions. They cannot translate costs of personnel into a payoff in service infusion.

Creating Metrics for Services

All the firms in our study tussled over metrics and measures for service performance. They had to adjust standard corporate outcome measures such as revenues, profits, and growth for services. Said one executive,

"We were asked to do things that make sense in a product company, but may not make sense in a service business—such as 'grow revenue next quarter by X percent'—we can't turn revenue on and off as quickly as with products; same with costs." The same executive said, "Financial people don't understand that you can't run a 'sale' on services to generate quick revenue given the long sales cycle and the fact that revenue doesn't come until service is delivered." Advocates of services and solutions must propose different measures altogether or suggest adaptations to product-oriented performance metrics for service divisions, units, and personnel.

Our firms described a wide variety of attempts to create service and solution metrics, and all but one company stated that measures are a thorny issue. Among the measures used are win–loss ratio on business, customer lifetime value, repeat business or renewal rate, and fill rate. Companies also used customer feedback measures such as customer satisfaction, customer loyalty, end-of-project reviews, and evaluations of collaboration with colleagues. Several of the companies studied also conducted formal quarterly business reviews with customers. Companies offering advisory services experimented with consulting industry measures such as chargeability (i.e., utilization of people and percent of time tied to clients), backlog of business (i.e., a measure that predicts future cash and profitability), new-in-year revenues, and ongoing revenue streams.

Perhaps the most promising metrics were clients' own measures of success, where firms and clients agreed upfront on desired outcomes of good performance and then evaluated success against those goals. In virtually all these situations, providers measured themselves by their customer's improved business performance. To illustrate, Rolls Royce offers "Total Care" service with its aircraft engines. The customer pays only for the hours the engine is in use. Rolls Royce takes responsibility for the engine's reliability and uptime. The popularity of these performance-based contracts is increasing: The customer pays its supplier based on performance against a jointly determined set of metrics.

Developing Value Propositions and Setting Prices

When goods-based companies develop their value propositions, they often start with the products they already make or distribute and then find customers who need these offerings. Communicating the value of an engine is easier than codifying the value of engine service: The former is often a one-time purchase with a set price, whereas the latter is often a series of payments over time in exchange for preventing far more costly downtime or damage. A pivotal issue is to explain to customers the benefits of a service or solution. One of our interviewees said, "You know what you get when you buy a product like 'crackers,' but you don't know what you get when you are buying a service" like in-store shelf management of the cracker category.

Related to the difficulty of developing value propositions is pricing. Goods-oriented firms are experienced at pricing tangibles, but not intangible services and solutions. Service pricing must fit customer perceptions of value, factor in costs—often largely labor—and set a figure that will encourage customers to use the service or solution.

Executives in our study frequently offered guarantees of cost savings, pay for performance, and gain sharing. These approaches all involve a mutual commitment to an outcome (e.g., saving a percent of costs) and then receiving partial or full compensation for meeting the outcome. If the provider meets or exceeds an outcome, both customer and company share in the gains, sometimes on an equal basis and sometimes on another agreed-upon basis.

Working with Partners

In some cases, opportunities along the infusion continuum require skills and resources outside the firm's capabilities and necessitate partnering with others. Several of our interviewees noted that they frequently used outside partners, particularly to offer services and solutions to the right on the continuum. Partnering allows greater flexibility. And, in some cases, the product firm further escalates its entry into a new service or solution by subsequently acquiring its former partner. One executive estimated that his company partners to access roughly half of its delivery resources. Some of the firms studied believe that partnering diminishes their control over outcomes, particularly over the level of service quality. For each partner, they need to agree upon clear metrics of performance, work out clear decision rights, and assign clear responsibility when customer problems occur. In addition, some companies are still uncomfortable sharing much information with potential partners.

Successful partnerships have a formula for the relationship, rather like a prenuptial agreement:

- Set clear expectations.
- Agree who owns the customer relationship.
- Define clear objectives and responsibilities.
- Clarify their company's standards and philosophy about service.
- Hold partners to these standards.
- Obtain feedback directly from customers about partner performance.
- Provide this feedback to partners, and
- Adjust accordingly, be it through additional training, reduced or increased compensation, lesser or greater responsibility, more aggressive growth goals, and so forth.

For Executive Discussion

Investing Strategically

1. How does senior management view service or solution development?
2. How can we make a strong case for investing in necessary personnel and other resources or partnerships to develop higher-level services and solutions?
3. Is there a partner who can help us to narrow the time to market and calculate the return on investment and the timing of revenues, based on that partner's experience providing similar services or solutions?
4. Is there a partner who can help us to develop services or solutions, where we can give them a greater share of revenues in exchange for knowledge and training?
5. How can we adjust our internal budgeting process to accommodate services and solutions? Can we adapt the one used for allocating overhead of shared services such as human resources or investor relations?
6. How can we adapt the language of capital investments and financial return for services and solutions?

Creating Metrics

1. How can we adjust our current corporate measures such as revenues, profits, and growth for service divisions, units, and personnel?
2. Might we adopt any of these common measures:
   - Win–loss ratio on business
   - Customer lifetime value
   - Repeat business or renewal rate
   - Fill rate
   - Customer satisfaction
   - Customer loyalty
   - End-of-project reviews
   - Evaluations of collaboration with colleagues
   - Formal quarterly business reviews with customers
   - Chargeability (i.e., utilization of people and percent of time tied to clients)
   - Backlog of business (i.e., a measure that predicts future cash and profitability)
   - New-in-year revenues
   - Ongoing revenue streams
   - Clients' own performance-based measures

Developing Value Propositions and Setting Prices

1. How can we explain our services and solutions to customers? Unlike products where we describe features and functionality, how can we articulate the benefits of our service or solution?
2. What price will fit customer perceptions of value, cover our costs, and encourage customers to use our service regularly? Can we offer a lower initial price in exchange for more customers who can help us to hone our capabilities?
3. To secure clients, might we offer guarantees of cost savings, pay for performance, and gain sharing?
4. Might we collaborate with customers to achieve an outcome (e.g., saving a percent of costs) in exchange for partial or full compensation for meeting that outcome?

Partnering

1. Can we leverage partners for specific skills and talent that we do not have or do not want to develop?
2. How can we structure such a partnership to maintain control over outcomes, particularly over the level of service quality?
3. How comfortable are we with sharing relevant information with partners so that our partnership might function more smoothly?
4. In contemplating the success of partnerships past, present, and future, did we or have we
   - Set clear expectations?
   - Agree who owns the customer relationship?
   - Define clear objectives and responsibilities?
   - Clarify their company's standards and philosophy about service?
   - Hold partners to these standards?
   - Obtain feedback directly from customers about partner performance?
   - Provide this feedback to partners?
   - Adjust training, compensation, responsibility, or other expectations accordingly?
5. If we answered no to any of the above, then we may have set ourselves up to fall short of our potential.
6. Can we pause and reset current partnerships so that expectations and accountabilities are more explicit?

CHAPTER 8

Conclusion

Cultivating a Service and Solution Culture

In this book, we provide a conceptual framework, the service infusion continuum, which enables managers within product-oriented firms to have strategic conversations about infusing services and solutions into their businesses. We give managers a means of talking about services and solutions ranging from those that support products (e.g., warranties) to those that support customers (e.g., integrated product–services solutions). We focus on the latter, and the key managerial constructs that change as companies work to offer these services and solutions. As managers strive to launch complex services and goods-service solutions, they will face different roadblocks that will require five types of significant change (i.e., 5 C's).

Companies on the service infusion journey can learn from each other by sharing their successful and unsuccessful practices within each of the Cs.

The most intractable aspect of service infusion is the entrenched product-oriented culture. The companies in our study emphasized the difficulty of changing the strongly held product mentality that underlies the firm's managerial strategies, practices, and processes—the silos, the hierarchy, the internal competition, and the tendency to hoard rather than share information. The leadership challenge is to convince the firm's top management and employees that service or solution success requires different strategies, values, and attitudes.

Developing services and solutions in goods-oriented organizations involves many strategic components, such as changing employee reward systems; altering management practices; and capturing and sharing employee and customer knowledge. The company must also offer service and solution positions that are paths to promotion so that employees have the opportunity to be as important as other employees. Employees must be customer advocates, key parties within the company must share customer information, and leaders must visibly and vocally promote a service philosophy. New services and solutions will fail without top management's support. One executive told us, "We have not valued the concept of being a great service provider."

Leaders must also enlist senior management and human resources teams in transitioning employees from goods to services and solutions. The transition is difficult: managers must lay down new career paths. Compensation, conditions for promotion, and other rewards and must tie key performance indicators to customer outcomes, not products' success. The career paths for services and solutions associates must be as rigorous, respected, and rewarding as those for product associates. Otherwise, the company's best talent will not commit to services or innovative customer-valued initiatives. One executive said, "This is really an issue of effective change management—in the beginning, we needed to convince our people that this is the right decision."

Key leaders must push for change and put the customer before the product. "Given our new organizational structure and matrix organization, there is a greater need for leaders whose style emphasizes teamwork and willingness to work to common goals across SBUs," said one manager. "Our current CEO is repositioning the company outward—his number one focus is enhancing the customer's experience. Our leaders' bonuses are tied in part to customer metrics and industry standards."

Culture is more than the sum of successful service and solution strategies and tactics. It involves companywide values, such as a customer focus, shared information, operational transparency, and employee parity, as well as actions that operationalize those values, such as busting silos, adjusting processes and performance metrics for services, and hiring, training, measuring, and rewarding employees according to customer-relevant goals.

Even if leaders align all five C's to generate service revenues, each move to the right on the continuum will require a shift in culture. Without significant cultural shifts, service infusion will stall.

For Executive Discussion

1. Have we fostered a sense of urgency around service infusion?
   - Have we examined our product market and competitive realities?
   - Have we identified and discussed potential crises or major opportunities in service infusion?
2. Have we identified all advocates of service infusion and formed a leadership coalition?
   - Does our coalition have enough organizational power to lead the transition to services and solutions?
   - How can we encourage these advocates to collaborate as a team?
3. Have we created a powerful vision of our future in services and solutions at the right hand of the continuum?
   - How can we use the service infusion continuum to help direct our change effort?
   - What short-term and long-term strategies will achieve our vision?
4. How are we communicating our vision of the service and solution–oriented organization?
   - Are we using every channel possible to communicate our vision?
   - Are we as a leadership team modeling new behaviors and setting new priorities?
5. Are we empowering our staff to act on the vision of service infusion?
   - In addition to the scorecard, what tools described in this book can we socialize to get started?
   - Which aspects of the five C's are the biggest obstacles to our organization? How shall we tackle them?
   - Which systems or structures are undermining our vision?

- How and where can we encourage risk taking and service-oriented ideas, experiments, and exploration?

6. What are some short-term wins, and how can we create and celebrate them?
   - How can we plan for visible performance improvement in service or solution development and delivery?
   - How can we drive such improvement?
   - How should we recognize and reward employees who contribute?

7. How can we consolidate and leverage improvements to expedite the transition?
   - Can we use our small wins and strong customer response to transform systems, structures, and policies that obstruct our vision?
   - Can we hire, promote, and develop employees who can implement new services and solutions?
   - How can we reinvigorate the process with new projects, partners, and customers as collaborators?

8. How can we institutionalize our new approaches and dismantle the product-oriented ones?
   - Can we articulate the connections between the new behaviors and organizational success in service infusion?
   - How can we ensure leadership development and succession?

APPENDIX 1

Research Approach, Resources, and Methodology

The overarching goal of the book is to identify and explain the challenges associated with companies transitioning from products to services and solutions. Once our goal was identified, we methodically worked toward understanding what was known about this phenomenon and how we could best make a contribution to business leaders. Early on in the process we discovered that there was an important piece missing in both the literature and in practice on the subject of service infusion. What was missing was a process to understand service infusion and its patterns and connections.[1] The development of a framework for service infusion became a priority in our work.

The Service Infusion Continuum is offered as a conceptual framework identifying and explicating the main challenges for product-oriented firms in growing services and solutions. The continuum helps describe dynamic factors associated with those challenges. We focus on business-to-business (B2B) firms because of the huge interest among product-dominant companies to infuse profitable services and solutions into their portfolio of offerings. We center on services and solutions that primarily support customers rather than the traditional entitlement services and other relatively less complex services that support products.

Our research approach rests on three pillars:

1. A synthesis of the existing service infusion literature,
2. The authors' extensive experience, and
3. An indepth study of five major corporations infusing services and solutions featuring interviews with high-level executives.

The approach allowed us to capture the most relevant contributions from leading experts in the field, leverage the deep and varied experience of the author team, and utilize the experiences of executives and managers leading blue-chip companies actively involved in infusing services in their organizations.

Literature Review

We first uncovered all the literature we could find related to service infusion, recognizing that some of this literature did not make any overt reference to infusion. We searched academic articles, textbooks, the business press, business books, conference proceedings, and corporate white papers related to service infusion. After an extensive review and analysis, we centered on over a hundred sources that best represented the literature.

We found that for some of the C's, the academic literature leads the practice of service infusion. For example, the literature on collaboration or co-creation with customers is developing quickly,[2] and yet the companies we studied consider collaboration to be limited to collecting customer information or—at most—involving customers only at the beginning of the service innovation process to understand their needs. Academic literature recognizes that customers consider solutions to involve relationships that extend from the development of solutions to their deployment.[3] The marketing literature offers insights for other C's as well. For capabilities, firms can learn from the literature on relationship marketing and consultative selling. For metrics, the vast marketing literature on customer satisfaction and loyalty, as well as the emerging literature on analytics, offers much for product-oriented firms.[4]

Other academic fields offer extensive research on topics such as organizational structure and culture. For example, company configurations appropriate in different types of firms, environments, and stages of change are studied in the fields of organizational behavior, industrial organization, and organizational change.[5] In the same fields, insights about organizational culture provides a foundation for understanding the myriad of factors associated with developing a strong services and solutions culture.

Many of our firms claimed that they benchmark other product-oriented firms that are infusing services. Just as fruitful might be benchmarking companies that have long been purely in the business of service. A 30-year history of research and practice on many of the same issues that companies discussed with us exists concerning pure service businesses.[6] Strategies for addressing these issues have been developed and refined. For example, service and solution businesses of all types have experimented with and learned appropriate metrics for measuring the success of individuals, units, divisions, and whole firms. Consulting and other professional service and solution firms have learned to measure, pay, motivate, and manage their personnel and businesses over time and these approaches can be adapted in product-oriented businesses. Service standardization and blueprinting have long been successfully deployed in service firms and can also be adapted for product-oriented firms.[7] More challenging to adapt, but still useful, are the strategies used to improve culture that successful customer-focused service firms such as Southwest Airlines, Zappos, USAA, The Ritz-Carlton Hotel, and Nordstrom use.[8]

Viewed as a whole, academic research on service infusion has been exploratory and has followed one of two approaches.[9] Some research has attempted to identify broad, strategic drivers of success in service infusion; other research has more narrowly focused on particular company strategies or tactics associated with transitioning to service.[10] Research dealing with issues related to service infusion has examined specific strategies including organizational structure, sales force characteristics, types of innovation, and, most recently, the key success factors for designing and delivering combinations of goods, services, and solutions such as hybrid offerings in business markets.[11]

Although past work has attempted to capture the dramatic shift to services and solutions by product-oriented companies, it lacks a framework for integration. Integrative work is needed to help managers effectively grow profitable service and solution revenues and to help researchers more deeply develop this area of focus. By studying the literature, we identify and explicate the domain of service infusion, the factors associated with the domain, and their relationships. These findings, in conjunction with our combined experience and a major research project, culminated with the service infusion continuum and this book.

Authors' Experience

Our work provides several broad conclusions regarding service infusion in practice. First, infusing services and solutions into a business is not a straightforward task, particularly for businesses that are steeped in manufacturing, technology, engineering, and product-oriented philosophies and practices—as were those we studied. Many companies are eager to move successfully along the path to services and solutions growth, and they want to learn from each other and from academics. Yet, even when the intent and commitment to services and solutions are well established, many impediments must be confronted. At the outset, we conjectured (based on our previous experience and research) that we would not find clear formulas for success. Our predictions were confirmed. Although we identified key issues and examples of approaches used by companies within each of our five C's, widely accepted practices or theories guiding this extremely important transformation do not yet exist. Thus, a primary outcome of the research from a managerial perspective was to capture what we know, present it in a useful way, and help managers begin a shared learning process with each other and with academics to move the domain forward. Experimentation with different approaches and learning based on the best practical and academic knowledge currently available can assist the leaders and pioneers of service infusion. We believe that the Service Infusion Continuum and five C's offer a valuable framework for sharing among companies and for additional research.

In addition to drawing on the literature, we also relied on our extensive combined experience gained through immersion over many years in related research, as well as consulting, executive teaching, and workshops with companies on the service infusion journey. The author team has over a century of experience to draw upon, and we have devoted our careers to research, teaching, and consulting in the areas of services and solutions strategy, management, and marketing. In addition to writing leading textbooks, more than two-dozen books, and over 200 articles, three of the authors are recipients of the American Marketing Association's prestigious annual Career Contributions to Services Marketing award. Each author is affiliated with the Center for Services Leadership in the W. P. Carey School of Business at Arizona State University and has worked closely with very early pioneers in service infusion and with many others who are just beginning the journey now.

Intensive Study of Several Companies

Our research also involved studying several companies primarily through indepth interviews with high-level executives in firms infusing services and solutions. This focus enabled us to explore and enhance the continuum as well as identify managerial insights, issues, and approaches within each of the service continuum's five C's. The interviews served as an important part of our research process by helping us understand managerial thinking and decision making surrounding service infusion.[12] Given the early stage of development of service infusion, we adopted a discovery-oriented, qualitative approach. Qualitative methods have been shown to be a strong foundation for understanding complex, emerging phenomena such as infusing services.

As the source of our interviews, we selected five Fortune 100 B2B companies that were in the process of infusing services and solutions. Each was a product-oriented company that had a division or more of its firm moving aggressively to incorporate services or solutions. The five companies represent the following industries: heavy equipment, health care supply, commercial building, aerospace, and diversified manufacturing. All the five companies have very long histories in manufacturing or distribution and all are relatively new to higher-valued services and solutions as a corporate strategy. For all of them, the transition from products to services and solutions represents a major cultural and organizational change.

In each business, we identified a lead executive who had either been directly involved in or was currently involved in forming the business unit to provide B2B services and solutions in his or her firm. This executive, in turn, identified four to six other executives or upper-level managers in the service division or divisions of the business to participate in the study. A total of 28 interviews were conducted across the five companies. A telephone interview of 90 minutes was arranged with each interviewee. In advance of the interview, each interviewee received an e-mail explaining the study and providing both the service infusion continuum, service offering definitions, and an interview guide containing a high-level set of questions to be discussed (see Appendix 2). The version of the interview guide sent in advance was limited to the general topics and did not contain the detailed probes that would later be asked by interviewers.

The interview guide contained open-ended questions of two types. First, we posed general questions about service infusion on topics such as the types of services and solutions the company offers or plans to offer; which services and solutions have been successful and unsuccessful; and the key lessons firms learned in transitioning to services and solutions. Next, we asked specific questions about each of the five dimensions, the five C's, which we identified in the literature review phase of the research.

The four researchers conducted all telephone interviews themselves, with two researchers on each call. Due to the strategic nature of the interviews, and to preserve confidentiality, the interviews were not recorded. Rather, in each interview, one researcher asked the questions while taking notes and the second researcher took more extensive notes on the answers to the questions. Thus, two sets of notes were available for each interview. These were then transcribed, reviewed by both researchers, and finalized as one integrated set of notes for each interviewee. Having two researchers involved in every interview allowed for a convergent perspective on the interviews to enhance the validity of the findings. The convergence helped empirically ground the findings and improve the chances of uncovering novel insights.[13]

After the interview results were compiled, individual interviews were analyzed to identify themes and the themes were then compared across interviews and companies, anchored on the original constructs, or five C's. This synthesis resulted in insights regarding the five constructs themselves as well as managerial insights into approaches used and challenges across the continuum and within the five C's. In exploring the five themes that we had identified in the literature review phase, we searched for similarities and differences resulting from specific firms being in different industries and at different stages of service infusion.[14] All of the notes were shared and reviewed by the four researchers with the goal of identifying challenges, managerial insights, and research issues for each construct within and across the sets of company interviews. The interviews also provided an opportunity to test and enhance the foundational service infusion framework and definitions that were developed in the first phase of the project.

Initial findings on the framework, challenges, and managerial insights were shared with the five companies in two webinars, one for executive sponsors, and one for all interviewees. This step allowed for clarification, validation, and enhancement of the framework and findings by study participants. The continual iteration between the framework, constructs, and data performed during the data analysis and sharing of the findings with the study participants allowed the researchers to achieve saturation, a point where the iteration process failed to yield substantial improvement to the framework or its implications.[15]

Finally, we describe the findings from the interviews with our participating companies using the five C's as an organizing framework. For each of the C's, we summarize the pivotal issues the companies described, the approaches the companies used to address the issues, and the key insights we gleaned. The result of these efforts were the ideas behind moving from products to services and solutions.

APPENDIX 2

Company Interview Guide

Questions

1. Does your organization currently offer or plan to offer—any of the services and solutions highlighted in black?
   (a) Which types of services on the continuum?
   (b) Please briefly describe these services and the value they bring to your customers.
2. In which of these services and solutions situations has the company been successful (give examples if possible)?
3. Looking across the continuum at the services that you do offer, what challenges have you faced in developing and delivering these services and solutions?
4. In what situations has the company *not* been successful to date?
5. What changes have you made to your organization in order to provide these services and solutions in addition to your products?
6. Have you used partners in delivering these services and solutions?
7. Have you found that new competencies and capabilities are needed to become successful in developing and delivering services and solutions across this continuum?
8. How have your customers participated in the provision, design, or development of any of the services shown in black on the figure?
9. How have you standardized services to become more efficient in delivering them? To what extent have you customized the services and solutions for individual clients?
10. How do you demonstrate the benefits associated with your services (or service-led solutions) to clients?
11. How challenging is it to communicate the value of your services and solutions through your pricing?
    To what extent do clients resist paying a fee for services?

12. Are there types of services and solutions that you are offering or planning to offer that we have not discussed? What are they?

13. Besides yourself, we are interviewing the following people in your organization. Are there other key individuals in the company that you believe we should talk to about the topics and issues we have discussed today?

About the Authors

All four authors have devoted their careers to research, teaching, and consulting in the areas of services strategy, management, and marketing. Three are recipients of the American Marketing Association's prestigious annual Career Contributions to Services Marketing Award. Each is affiliated with the Center for Services Leadership in the W. P. Carey School of Business at Arizona State University.

Valarie A. Zeithaml was one of the co-authors of *Delivering Quality Service*, the 1990 business book that introduced the Gaps Model of Service Quality and SERVQUAL, a multidimensional scale for assessing customer perceptions of service quality. Her research, which has won awards in *Journal of Marketing, Journal of Marketing Research, Journal of Consumer Research*, and *Journal of Service Research*, primarily deals with the topics of service quality, customer equity, customer perceived value, and service infusion. In total, she has 40,000 citations in business, academic, and other publications.

Dr. Zeithaml is the David S. Van Pelt Family Distinguished Professor of Marketing and an award-winning teacher and researcher at the Kenan-Flagler Business School at the University of North Carolina. She was honored with the 2009 Sheth Foundation or *Journal of Marketing* Award for scholarship based on the benefits of time and hindsight, the 2009 AMA Irwin/McGraw-Hill Distinguished Marketing Educator Award for lifetime leadership in marketing education and extensive contributions to the marketing discipline, and the 2008 Paul D. Converse Award for enduring contributions through a body of work. Zeithaml and her co-authors have written three books: *Driving Customer Equity: How Customer Lifetime Value is Reshaping Corporate Strategy, Delivering Quality Service*, and the textbook entitled *Services Marketing*.

Stephen W. Brown co-authored the lead article in a 2005 issue of the *Journal of Service Research* on forming successful services in product-oriented firms. A related article was published in the *Journal of Service Management* in 2008. He is also the lead author of the *Wall Street Journal* article from June 22, 2009, "Beyond Products: More Manufacturers are Branching out into Service Business." His primary research and executive and MBA teaching focus throughout his career has been on service strategy and marketing.

Dr. Brown is the Emeritus Edward M. Carson Chair, Professor of Marketing Emeritus and Distinguished Faculty with the Center for Services Leadership at Arizona State University's W. P. Carey School of Business. He served as the CSLs founding executive director from 1985 to 2011. He is also a Strategic Partner with The INSIGHT Group, a consulting organization focused on helping its clients grow services and solutions. Professor Brown is a former national president of the American Marketing Association. He has co-authored and co-edited 23 books and over 100 articles on services and service-related topics. He has been identified as one of the 10 most frequent contributors to the English-language services marketing literature in the world. He has been awarded honorary doctoral degrees from universities in Finland and Sweden, and he received the Educator of the Year award from the Association for Service Management International.

Dr. Brown serves as a speaker and workshop leader for conferences and business meetings around the world, most often featuring his work in helping product-oriented companies successfully grow profitable services revenue. Brown has co-founded three companies, and he serves on the board of directors of several corporations and a nonprofit organization.

Mary Jo Bitner has written extensively on service marketing and management topics including satisfaction with services, customer–employee interactions, service blueprinting, and service infusion. Her work is published in leading journals including *Journal of Marketing, Journal of Service Research, Journal of Marketing Research*, and *California Management Review*, among others. Her research and MBA teaching throughout her career have focused on service management and marketing.

Dr. Bitner is Professor of Marketing, Edward M. Carson Chair in Services Marketing, and Executive Director of the Center for Services Leadership in the W. P. Carey School of Business, Arizona State University. She has contributed over two decades of research to the field of services marketing. Professor Bitner has published more than 45 journal articles relevant to service management and marketing in leading academic and managerial journals. Her current research focuses on helping product-oriented companies infuse service growth strategies. Dr. Bitner was honored with the AMA-SERVSIG Career Contributions Award for contributions to the discipline, an IBM Faculty Fellowship award for her pioneering contributions to the field, and with the inaugural ISSIP Fellow Award for Lifetime Achievement in Service Science. She is co-author with Valarie Zeithaml and Dwayne Gremler of *Services Marketing: Integrating Customer Focus Across the Firm* (McGraw-Hill, 6th edition, 2013), a prominent text in services that is used at universities worldwide. Bitner served on the Board of Directors of the American Marketing Association and is the editor in chief (2013 to 2017) of the *Journal of Service Research*, the top-rated academic journal for service research globally.

Jim Salas is an Assistant Professor of Marketing in the Graziadio School of Business and Management at Pepperdine University. His main research is focused on the implementation of service infusion strategies among traditional industrial manufacturers. His research was sponsored by the Center for Services Leadership at ASU, where he won several teaching awards. Prior to his studies at ASU, Professor Salas spent more than a decade at AT&T in corporate sales where he held several sales management and consulting positions. Salas is a member of the PhD Project, American Marketing Association, and Academy of Marketing Science. He has presented his work at academic conferences and at multinational corporations. Currently Salas leads an international research team working extensively with a leading European technology company in implementing service infusion strategies.

Notes

Preface

1. Fang, Palmatier, and Steenkamp (2008).
2. MacInnis (2011).

Chapter 1

1. *Oxford Economics* (2013).
2. Eggert, Hogreve, Ulaga, and Muenkhoff (2011).
3. Ulaga and Reinhartz (2011).
4. Neu and Brown (2005).
5. Weigand (2013, June).
6. Penttinen and Saarinen (2005).
7. *Oxford Economics* (2013).

Chapter 2

1. General Electric (2010, 2011, and 2012).
2. Xerox (n.d.).
3. Xerox (2013, August).
4. Allmendinger and Lombreglia (2005).
5. Allmendinger and Lombreglia (2005).
6. Kubr(2002).
7. IBM (n.d.).
8. Tuli, Kohli, and Bharadwaj (2007).
9. Tuli, Kohli, and Bharadwaj (2007); Neu and Brown (2005).
10. Swaminathan (2001), along with our own research.
11. Ulaga and Reinhartz (2011), Storbacka (2011).
12. Tuli, Kohli, and Bharadwaj (2007); Sawhney, Balasurbramanian, and Krishnan (2005); Epp and Price (2011); Edvardsson et al. (2005); Alam (2002).
13. Gronroos (1990).

Chapter 3

1. Siemens (n.d.).
2. Ploetner (2008).
3. Oliva and Kallenberg (2003).
4. Neu and Brown (2008).
5. Snehota and Hakansson (1995); Neu and Brown (2008).
6. Neu and Brown (2008).
7. Hodgson-Lyons (2013).
8. Gebauer, Edvardsson, Gustafsson, and Witell (2010).
9. Ploetner (2008).
10. Ploetner (2008); Jacob, Plotner, and Zedler (2005).
11. Shah, Rust, Parasuraman, Staelin, and Day (2005).
12. Day (1999).
13. Gulati (2007).
14. Sawhney, Balasubramanian, and Krishnan (2005).

Chapter 4

1. Osram Sylvania (August, 2013).
2. Weitz and Bradford (1999).
3. Shapiro and Varian (1999).
4. Reinartz and Ulaga (2008).
5. Neu and Brown (2005).
6. Sheth and Sharma (2008),
7. Vargo and Lusch (2004)
8. Davies,Brady, and Hobday (2005)
9. Weitz and Bradford (1999).
10. Tuli, Kohli, and Bharadwaj (2007).
11. Galbraith (2002); Sheth and Sharma (2008).
12. Sharma and Malloy (1999); Ronchetto, Hutt, and Reingen (1989).
13. Steward, Hutt, Walker, and Kumar (2009).
14. Johansson, Krishnamurthy, and Schlissberg (2007); Davies, Brady, and Hobday (2007); Homburg, Workman, and Jensen (2002).
15. Cornet, Katz, Molloy, Schadler, Sharma, and Tipping (2000); Gulati (2007); Krishnamurthy, Johansson, and Schlissberg (2003).
16. Our research, as well as Homburg and Jensen (2007); Homburg, Jensen, and Hrohmer (2008); Malshe (2010).
17. Neu and Brown (2005); Donavan, Brown, and Mower, (2004); Challagalla, Venkatesh, and Kohli (2009).
18. Davies, Brady, and Hobday (2005).

Chapter 5

1. Waller (2013, April).
2. Pearson (2013, May).
3. King (2013, July).
4. Tuli, Kohli, and Bharadwaj (2007).
5. Tuli, Kohli, and Bharadwaj (2007).
6. Bulkeley (2009).
7. Davies, Brady, and Hobday (2005).
8. Levitt (1975).
9. Davies, Brady, and Hobday (2005).
10. Auguste, Harmon, and Pandit (2005).
11. Auguste, Harmon, and Pandit (2005).
12. Fagan, Harmon, and Lukes (2007).
13. Fagan, Harmon, and Lukes (2007).
14. Hyotylainen and Moller (2007).

Chapter 6

1. Tuli, Kohli, and Bharadwaj (2007); Sawhney, Balasubramanian, and Krishnan (2005).
2. Edvardsson, Gustafsson, Kristensson, Magnusson, and Matthing (2005).
3. Hauser, Tellis, and Griffin (2005); Hoyer, Chandy, Dorotic, Kraft, and Singh (2010).
4. Vargo and Lusch (2004); Grönroos (2011).
5. Grönroos (2011).
6. Meuter, Bitner, Ostrom, and Brown(2005).
7. Chan, Yim, and Lam (2010); Epp and Price (2011); Zeithaml, Wilson, Bitner, and Gremler (2012).
8. Alam(2002); Hauser, Tellis, and Griffin (2005); Edvardsson, Gustafsson, Kristensson, Magnusson, and Matthing (2005); Bettencourt (2010); Ramaswamy and Gouillart (2010).
9. For example, Henard and Szymanski (2001).
10. For exceptions, see Cova and Salle (2008); Payne, Storbacka, and Frow (2008); Grönroos and Helle (2010); Bettencourt, Ostrom, Brown, and Roundtree (2002).
11. Fang (2008a); Homburg, Muller, and Klarmann (2011).
12. Epp and Price (2011).
13. Ordanini and Parasuraman (2011).
14. For example, Chan, Yim, and Lam (2010); Prahalad and Ramaswamy (2004); Fang, Palmatier, and Evans (2008b).

15. Fang (2008a); Homburg, Muller, and Klarmann (2011).
16. Homberg, Muller, and Klarmann (2011).

Chapter 7

1. Friedman (2013, September).
2. Friedman (2013, September).

Appendix 1

1. MacInnis (2011).
2. For example, Etgar (2008).
3. For example, Tuli, Kohli, and Bharadwaj (2007).
4. For example, Zeithaml, Parasuraman, and Berry (1995).
5. For example, Galbraith (2002).
6. Zeithaml, Wilson, Bitner, and Gremler (2012); Zeithaml and Parasuraman (2004).
7. Bitner, Ostrom, and Morgan (2008).
8. Bloomberg Business Week (2010).
9. For notable exceptions, see Fang, Palmatier, and Steenkamp (2008); and Ulaga and Reinhartz (2011).
10. For example, Fang, Palmatier, and Steenkamp (2008); Neu and Brown (2005).
11. Galbraith (2002); Oliva and Kallenburg (2003); Neu and Brown (2008), Tuli, Kohli, and Bharadwaj (2007); Sheth and Sharma (2008); Neu and Brown (2005); Gebauer (2008); Bolton, Grewal, and Levy (2007); Ulaga and Reinartz (2011).
12. Jaworski (2011).
13. Eisenhardt (1989).
14. Eisenhardt (1989).
15. Eisenhardt (1989).

References

Alam, I. Summer 2002. "An Exploratory Investigation of User Involvement in New Service Development." *Journal of the Academy of Marketing Science* 30, no. 3, pp. 250–251.

Allmendinger, G.; and R. Lombreglia. October 2005. "Four Strategies for the Age of Smart Services." *Harvard Business Review* 83, no. 10, pp. 131–145.

Auguste, B.G.; E.P. Harmon; and V. Pandit. 2005. "The Right Services Strategies for Product Companies." *McKinsey Quarterly* 1, pp. 40–51.

Bettencourt, L.; A.L. Ostrom; S.W. Brown.; and R.I. Roundtree. Summer 2002. "Client Co-production in Knowledge-Intensive Business Services." *California Management Review* 44, no. 4, pp. 100–128.

Bettencourt, L.A. 2010. *Service Innovation: How to Go from Customer Needs to Breakthrough Services.* London, UK: McGraw-Hill.

Bitner, M.J.; A.L. Ostrom; and F.N. Morgan. May 2008, "Service Blueprinting: A Practical Technique for Service Innovation." *California Management Review* 50, no. 3, pp. 55–94.

Bloomberg Business Week. 2010. *World Class Customer Service.* http://images.businessweek.com/ss/10/02/0218_customer_service_champs/1.htm

Bolton, R.N.; D. Grewal; and M. Levy. March 2007. "Six Strategies for Competing Through Services: An Agenda for Future Research." *Journal of Retailing* 83, no. 1, pp. 1–4.

Bulkeley, W.M. February 24, 2009. "Xerox Tries to Go beyond Copiers." *The Wall Street Journal Online.*

Challagalla, G.; R. Venkatesh; and A.K. Kohli. March 2009. "Proactive Postsales Service: When and Why Does it Pay Off?" *Journal of Marketing* 73, pp. 70–87.

Chan, K.W.; C.K.B. Yim; and S.S.K. Lam. May 2010. "Is Customer Participation in Value Creation a Double-Edged Sword? Evidence from Professional Financial Services Across Cultures." *Journal of Marketing* 74, no. 3, pp. 48–54.

Cornet, E.; R. Katz; R. Molloy; J. Schadler; D. Sharma; and A. Tipping. November 2000. *Customer Solutions: From Pilots to Profits.* 1–15. New York, NY: Booz-Allen & Hamilton Inc.

Cova, B.; and R. Salle. May 2008. "Marketing Solutions in Accordance with the S-D Logic: Co-creating Value with Customer Network Actors." *Industrial Marketing Management* 37, no. 3, pp. 270–277.

Davies, A.; T. Brady; and M. Hobday. February 2007. "Organizing for Solutions: Systems Seller vs. Systems Integrator." *Industrial Marketing Management* 36, no. 2, pp. 183–193.

Davies, A.; T. Brady; and M. Hobday. Spring 2005. "Charting a Path Toward Integrated Solutions." *Sloan Management Review* 47, no. 3, pp. 39–48.

Day, G.S. 1999. *The Market Driven Organization: Understanding, Attracting, and Keeping Valuable Customers.* New York, NY: Simon and Schuster Inc.

Donavan, T.; T.J. Brown; and J.C. Mowen. January 2004. "Internal Benefits of Service-Worker Customer Orientation: Job Satisfaction, Commitment, and Organizational Citizenship Behaviors." *Journal of Marketing* 68, no. 1, pp. 128–146.

Edvardsson, B.; A. Gustafsson; P. Kristensson; P. Magnusson; and J. Matthing. 2005. *Involving Customers in New Service Development.* London: Imperial College Press.

Eggert, A.; J. Hogreve; W. Ulaga; and E. Muenkhoff. 2011."Revenue and Profit Implications of Industrial Service Strategies." Working Book. Paterborn, Germany: University of Paderborn.

Eisenhardt, K. October 1989. "Building Theories from Case Study Research." *Academy of Management Review* 14, no. 4, pp. 532–550.

Epp, A.M.; and L.L. Price. March 2011. "Designing Solutions Around Customer Network Identity Goals." *Journal of Marketing* 75, no. 2, pp. 35–54.

Etgar, M. March 2008. "A Descriptive Model of the Consumer Co-production Process." *Journal of the Academy of Marketing Science* 36, no. 1, pp. 97–108.

Fagan, T.; E. Harmon; and T. Lukes. February 2007. "Improving Productivity in Product Services." *The McKinsey Quarterly,* pp. 1–5.

Fang, E; R.W. Palmatier; and J.-B.E.M. Steenkamp. September 2008. "Effect of Service Transition Strategies on Firm Value." *Journal of Marketing* 72, no. 5, pp. 1–14.

Fang, E. July 2008a. "Customer Participation and the Trade-off Between New Product Innovativeness and Speed to Market." *Journal of Marketing* 72, no. 4, pp. 90–104.

Fang, E; R.W. Palmatier; and K.R. Evans. September 2008b."Influence of Customer Participation on Creating and Sharing of New Product Value." *Journal of the Academy of Marketing Science* 36, no. 3, pp. 322–335.

Friedman, T.L. September 2013. "When Complexity Is Free." *New York Times.*

Galbraith, J.R. Autumn 2002. "Organizing to Deliver Solutions." *Organizational Dynamic* 21, no. 2, 194–207.

Gebauer, H. January–May 2008. "Identifying Service Strategies in Product Manufacturing Companies by Exploring Environment Strategy Configurations." *Industrial Marketing Management* 37, no. 3, pp. 278–291.

Gebauer, H.; B. Edvardsson; A. Gustafsson; and L. Witell. May 2010. "Match or Mismatch: Strategy-Structure Configurations in the Service Business of Manufacturing Companies." *Journal of Service Research* 13 , no. 2, pp. 198–215.

General Electric. 2010. *Annual Reports.*

General Electric. 2012. *Annual Report.*

Gerenal Electric. 2011. *Annual Report.*

Gerstner, L.V. 2002. *Who Said Elephants Can't Dance? Inside IBM's Historic Turnaround.* London: Harper Collins Publishers.

Gronroos, C. January 1990. "Relationships Approach to Marketing in Service Context: The Marketing and Organizational Behavior Interface." *Journal of Business Research* 20, no. 1, pp. 3–11.

Grönroos, C. September 2011. "Value Co-creation of Service Logic: A Critical Analysis." *Marketing Theory* 11, no. 3, pp. 279–301.

Grönroos, C.; and P. Helle. March 2010. "Adopting a Service Logic in Manufacturing: Conceptual Foundation and Metrics for Mutual Value Creation." *Journal of Service Management,* 21, no. 5, 554–590.

Gulati, R. May 2007. "Silo Busting: How to Execute on the Promise of Customer Focus." *Harvard Business Review* 85, no. 5, pp. 1–9.

Hauser, J.; G.J. Tellis; and A. Griffin. November 2005. "Research on Innovation: A Review and Agenda for Marketing Science." *Marketing Science* 25, no. 6, pp. 687–717.

Henard, D.H.; and D.M. Szymanski. August 2001. "Why Some New Products are More Successful Than Others." *Journal of Marketing Research* 38, no. 3, pp. 362–375.

Hodgson-Lyons, D. May 21, 2013. "Changing a Product Company's Culture and Business Model." *Session at the Annual Conference of the Strategic Account Management Association.* Hollywood, FL: Strategic Account Management Association Inc.

Homburg, C.; J.P. Workman; and O. Jensen. April 2002. "A Configurational Perspective on Key Account Management." *Journal of Marketing* 66, no. 2, pp. 38–60.

Homburg, C.; M. Muller; and M. Klarmann. March 2011. "When Should the Customer Really be King? On the Optimum Level of Customer Orientation in Sales Encounters." *Journal of Marketing* 75, no. 2, pp. 55–74.

Homburg, C; and O. Jensen. July 2007. "The Thought Worlds of Marketing and Sales: Which Differences Make a Difference?" *Journal of Marketing* 71, no. 3, pp. 124–142.

Homburg, C.; O. Jensen; and H. Hrohmer. March 2008."Configurations of Marketing and Sales: A Taxonomy." *Journal of Marketing* 72, no. 2, pp. 133–154.

Hoyer, W.D.; R. Chandy; M. Dorotic; M. Kraft; and S.S. Singh. August 2010."Consumer Cocreation in New Product Development." *Journal of Service Research* 13, no. 3, pp. 283–296.

Hyotylainen, M.; and K. Moller. 2007. "Service Packaging: Key to Successful Provisioning of ICT Business Solutions." *Journal of Services Marketing* 21, no. 2, pp. 304–312.

IBM. n.d. Website (accessed August, 2013). http://www.businessweek.com/stories/2006-09-26/ibm-pushes-service-products-businessweek-business-news-stock-market-and-financial-advice

Jacob, F.; O. Plötner; and C.L. Zedler. 2006. "Competence Commercialization von Industrieunternehmen: Phänomen, Elinordnung und Forschungsfragen." *ESCP-EAP Working Book Nr. 17.*

Jaworski, B.J. July 2011."On Managerial Relevance." *Journal of Marketing* 75, no. 4, pp. 211–224.

Johansson, J.E.; C. Krishnamurthy; and H.E. Schlissberg. 2007. "Solving the Solutions Problem." *The McKinsey Quarterly* 3, pp. 3–7.

King, I. July 2013. "Pearson's Step Forward; Business Editor's Commentary." *The Times.*

Krishnamurthy, C.; J. Johansson; and H. Schlissberg. April 2003. "Solutions Selling: Is the Pain worth the Gain?" *McKinsey Marketing Solutions* 1, no. 1, pp. 1–13.

Kubr, M. 2002. *Management Consulting—A Guide to the Profession*, 4th ed. Geneva: International Labour Office.

Levitt, T. 1975. "The Industrialization of Service." *Harvard Business Review* 54, no. 5, pp. 53–74.

MacInnis D.J. July 2011, "A Framework for Conceptual Contributions in Marketing." *Journal of Marketing* 75, no. 4, pp. 135–154.

Malshe, A. January 2010. "How is Marketers' Credibility Construed Within the Sales-Marketing Interface?" *Journal of Business Research* 63, no. 1, 13–19.

Meuter, M.L.; M.J. Bitner; A.L. Ostrom; and S.W. Brown. April 2005."Choosing Among Alternative Service Delivery Modes an Investigation of Customer Trail of Self-Service Technologies." *Journal of Marketing* 69, no. 2, pp. 61–83.

Neu, W.A.; and S.W. Brown. August 2005."Forming Successful Business to Business Services in Goods-Oriented Firms." *Journal of Service Research* 8, no. 1, pp. 3–7.

Neu, W.A.; and S.W. Brown.2008. "Manufacturers Forming Successful Complex Business Services: Designing an Organization to Fit the Market." *International Journal of Service Industry Management* 19, no. 2, pp. 232–251.

Oliva, R.; and R. Kallenberg. 2003."Managing the Transition from Products to Services." *International Journal of Service Industry Management* 14, no. 2, pp. 150–172.

Ordanini, A.; and A. Parasuraman. February 2011. "Service Innovation Viewed Through a Service-oriented Logic Lens: A Conceptual Framework and Empirical Analysis." *Journal of Service Research* 14, no. 1, pp. 3–23.

Osram Sylvania. 2013. "About SYLVANIA Lighting Services." *Osram Sylvania Services.* Osram AG: http://www.sylvania.com/en-us/services/about-sls/Pages/default.aspx

Oxford Economics. 2013. *Manufacturing Transformation.*

Payne, A.F.; K. Storbacka; and P. Frow. March 2008. "Managing the Co-creation of Value." *Journal of the Academy of Marketing Science* 35, no. 1, pp. 83–95.

Pearson. May 2013. Website. http://www.strategy-business.com/article/18411?pg=all&tid=27782251

Penttinen, E.; and T. Saarinen. 2005. "Opportunities and Challenges for B2B Manufacturing Firms: Moving from Products to Services-Case SKF." In *Managing Business in a Muliti-Chanel World: Success Factors for E-Business,* eds. Saarinen; Tinnila and Tseng. Idea Group Inc.

Ploetner, O. 2008. "The Development of Consulting in Goods-Based Companies." *Industrial Marketing Management* 37, no. 3, pp. 329–338.

Prahalad, D.K.; and V. Ramaswamy. 2004. *The Future of Competition: Co-creating Unique Value with Customers.* Boston, MA: Harvard Business School Press.

Ramaswamy, V.; and F. Gouillart. October 2010. "Building the Co-creative Enterprise." *Harvard Business Review* 88, no. 10, pp. 100–109.

Reinartz, W. and W. Ulaga. May 2008."How to Sell Services More Profitably." *Harvard Business Review* 85, no. 5, pp. 90–95.

Ronchetto, J.; M.D. Hutt; and P.H. Reingen. October 1989. "Embedded Influence Patterns in Organizational Buying Systems." *The Journal of Marketing* 53, no. 4, pp. 51–62.

Sawhney, M.; S. Balasubramanian; and V.V. Krishnan. 2005."Going Beyond the Product: Defining, Designing, and Delivering Customer Solutions." In *The Service-oriented Logic of Marketing: Dialog, Debate, and Directions,* eds. R.F. Lusch; and S.L. Vargo, pp. 356–380. New York, NY: M.E. Sharpe.

Shah, D.; R.T. Rust; A. Parasuraman; R. Staelin; and G.S. Day. November 2005. "The Path to Customer Centricity." *Journal of Service Research* 9, no. 2, pp. 114–124.

Shapiro, C.; and H.R. Varian. 1999. *Information Rules: A Strategic Guide to the Network Economy.* Cambridge: Harvard Business School Press, Print.

Sharma, D.; and R. Molloy. 1999. *The Truth About Customer Solutions.* Virginia, DC: Booz-Allen & Hamilton.

Sheth, J.N.; and A. Sharma. May 2008. "The Impact of the Product of Service Shift in Industrial Markets and the Evolution of the Sales Organization." *Industrial Management* 37, no. 3, pp. 260–269.

Siemens n.d. http://www.siemens.com/corp/en/siemens_websites_worldwide. htm; https://www.smc.siemens.de/en/smc-global/smc-at-a-glance/; http:// www.siemens.com/investor/pool/en/investor_relations/siemens_ar_2012. pdf; http://dealbook.nytimes.com/2010/12/15/siemens-to-sell-it-unit-to-atos-for-1-1-billion/?_r=0 (accessed August, 2013).

Snehota, I.; and H. Hakansson. 1995. *Developing Relationships in Business Networks.* London: Routledge.

Steward, M.D.; M.D. Hutt; B.A. Walker; and A. Kumar. 2009."Role Identity and Attributions of High-performing Salespeople." *Journal of Business & Industrial Marketing* 24, no. 7, pp. 463–473.

Storbacka, K. July 2011. "A Solution Business Model: Capabilities and Management Practice for Integrated Solutions." *Industrial Marketing Management* 40, no. 5, pp. 699–711.

Swaminathan J.M. Spring 2001. "Using Standardized Operations." *California Management Review* 43, no. 3, pp. 125–135.

Tuli, K.R.; A.K. Kohli; and S.G. Bharadwaj. July 2007. "Rethinking Customer Solutions: From Product Bundles to Relational Processes." *Journal of Marketing* 71, no. 3, pp. 1–17.

Ulaga, W; and W. Reinartz. November 2011. "Hybrid Offerings: How Manufacturing Firms Combines Goods and Services Successfully." *Journal of Marketing* 75, no. 6, pp.5–23.

Vargo, S.L. and R.F. Lusch. January 2004. "Evolving to a New Dominant Logic for Marketing." *Journal of Marketing* 68, no. 1, 1–17.

Waller, M. April 2013. "Profits in Education." *The Times.*

Weigand, J.R. June 2013. *The Journey of a Services Business in a 210 Year Old Products-Based Company*, QUIS 13 Symposium. Karlstad, Sweden: University of Karlstad.

Weitz, B.A.; and K.D. Bradford. Spring 1999. "Personal Selling and Sales Management: A Relationship Marketing Perspective." *Journal of the Academy of Marketing Science* 27, no. 2, pp. 241–254.

Xerox. August 2013. *Analysis of Instructions to Endpoint Conductors on Envelops Addressed to Train Earnings Reports*, Amtrak/Xerox Revenue Operations, Six Founders Boulevard, Suite E, El Paso, TX 79906. Café Car, Amtrak train 48.

Xerox. n.d. *City of Riverside–Print Governance Case Study*,http://www.consulting. xerox.com/case-studies/city-of-riverside-governance/enus.html (accessed October 2013).

Zeithaml, V.A.; and A. Parasuraman. 2004. *Service Quality, MSI Relevant Knowledge Series*. Cambridge, MA: Marketing Science Institute.

Zeithaml, V.A.; L.L. Berry; and A. Parasuraman. April 1996. "The Behavioral Consequences of Service Quality." *Journal of Marketing* 60, no. 2, 31–46.

Zeithaml, V.A.; A. Wilson; M.J. Bitner; and D. Gremler. 2012. *Services Marketing: Balancing Customer Expectations and Perceptions Across the Firm*, 6th ed. New York, NY: McGraw Hill.

Additional Resources

Anand, B.N.; and T. Khanna. March 2000. "Do Firms Learn to Create Value? The Case of Alliances." *Strategic Management Journal* 21, no. 3, pp. 295–315.

Anderson, E. 2005. "Organizing for Customer-Centric Marketing." *Forrester Report*, http://forrester.com (accessed July 7, 2005).

Anderson, J.C.; J.A. Narus; and W. vanRossum. March 2006. "Customer Value Propositions in Business Markets." *Harvard Business Review* 84, no. 3, pp. 90–99.

Bennett, J.; S. Deven; and A. Tipping. 2001. "Customer Solutions: Building a Strategically Aligned Business Model." http://www.boozallen.com/media/file/76878.pdf (accessed August 2009).

Bharadwaj, S.G.; P.R. Varadarajan; and J. Fahy. October 1993. "Sustainable Competitive Advantage in Service Industries: A Conceptual Model and Research." *Journal of Marketing* 57, no. 4, pp. 83–99.

Billington, J. April 1997, "How to Customize for the Real World." *Harvard Management Update* 2, no. 4, pp. 1–3.

Bitner, M.J.; A.L. Ostrom; and F.N. Morgan. Spring 2008. "Service Blueprinting: A Practical Guide for Service Innovation." *California Management Review* 50, no. 3, pp. 66–94.

Bitner, M.J.; and S.W. Brown. January–February 2008, "The Service Imperative." *Business Horizons* 51, no. 1, pp. 39–46.

Brady, T.; A. Davies; and D. Gann. 2005. "Creating Value by Delivering Integrated Solutions." *International Journal of Project Management* 23, no. 5, pp. 360–365.

Brown, S.W.; A. Gustafsson; and L. Witell. 2011. "Service Logic: Transforming Product-Focused Businesses." White Paper, Center for Services Leadership, W. P. Carey School of Business, Arizona State University.

Brown, S.W.; A. Gustafsson; and L. Witell. June 2009. "Beyond Products: More Manufacturers are Branching out into Service Business," *The Wall Street Journal*, R7.

Cohen, M.A.; N. Agrawal; and V. Agrawal. May 2006. "Winning in the Aftermarket." *Harvard Business Review* 84, pp. 129–138.

Day, G.S. January 2004. "Invited Commentaries on Evolving to a New Dominant Logic for Marketing." *Journal of Marketing* 68, no. 1, pp. 18–27.

Dubey, A.; and D. Wagle. 2007. "Delivering Software as a Service." *The McKinsey Quarterly*, http://www.mckinseyquarterly.com/Delivering_software_as_a_service_2006 (accessed May 2007).

Edvardsson, B.; M. Holmlund; and T. Strandvik. May 2008."Initiation of Business Relationships in Service-Dominant Settings." *Industrial Marketing Management* 37, no. 3, pp. 339–350.

Flint, D.J.; R.B. Woodruff; and S.F. Gardial. October 2002."Exploring the Phenomenon of Customers' Desired Value Change in a Business-to-Business Context." *Journal of Marketing* 55, no. 4, pp. 102–117.

Foote, N.W.; J. Galbraith; Q. Hope; and D. Miller. Autumn 2001."Making Solutions the Answer." *McKinsey Quarterly*, 31, no. 3, pp. 194–207.

Frei, F.X. April 2008. "The Four Things a Service Business Must Get Right." *Harvard Business Review* 86, no. 4, pp. 70–80.

Gebauer, H. 2012. *Services Business Development in Capital Goods Manufacturing Companies*, forthcoming Book Manuscript.

Gebhardt, G.F.; G.S. Carpenter; and J.F. Jr. Sherry. October 2005. "Creating a Market Orientation: A Longitudinal, Multi-firm, Grounded Analysis of Cultural Transformation." *Journal of Marketing* 70, no. 4, pp. 37–55.

Glaser, B.; and A. Strauss. 1957. *The Discovery of Grounded Theory*. Chicago, IL: Aldine.

Hamm, S. September 26, 2006. "IBM Pushes Service Products." *BusinessWeek*, http://www.businessweek.com/technology/content/sep2006/tc20060926_250921.htm (accessed September 2006).

Heskett, J.L.; W.E. Sasser; and L.A. Schlesinger. 1997. *The Service Profit Chain*. New York, NY: The Free Press.

Houston, M.B.; B.A. Walker; M.D. Hutt; and P.H. Reingen. April 2001. "Cross-Unit Competition for a Market Charter: The Enduring Influence of Structure." *Journal of Marketing* 65, no. 2, pp. 19–34.

Jacob, F.; and W. Ulaga. May 2008. "The Transition from Product to Service in Business Markets: An Agenda for Academic Inquiry." *Industrial Marketing Management* 37, no. 3, pp. 247–253.

Kohli, A.; and B. Jaworski. April 1990. "Market Orientation: The Construct, Research Propositions, and Managerial Implications." *Journal of Marketing* 54, no. 2, pp. 1–18.

Lohr, S. January 19, 2010. "Huge Payoff for I.B.M. After a Shift." *The New York Times*, http://www.nytimes.com/2010/01/20/technology/companies/20blueweb.html (accessed January 22).

Lusch, R.F.; S.L. Vargo; and M. O'Brien. March 2007."Competing Through Service: Insights from Service-Dominant Logic." *Journal of Retailing* 83, no. 1, pp. 5–18.

Matthyssens, P.; and K. Vandenbempt. 2010. "Service Addition as Business Market Strategy: Identification of Transition Trajectories." *Journal of Service Management* 21, no. 5, pp. 693–714.

Matthyssens, P.; and K. Vandenbempt. May 2008. "Moving from Basic Offerings to Value-Added Solutions: Strategies, Barriers and Alignment." *Industrial Marketing Management* 37, no. 3, pp. 316–328.

Moorman, C.; and A.S. Miner. February 1998. "The Impact of Organizational Memory on New Product Performance and Creativity." *Journal of Marketing Research* 34, no. 1, pp. 91–105.

Morgan, N.; E.W. Anderson; and V. Mittal. July 2005. "Understanding Firms' Customer Satisfaction Information Usage." *Journal of Marketing* 59, no. 3, pp. 131–151.

Ng, I.C.L.; and S.S. Nudurupati. March 2010. "Outcome-Based Service Contracts in the Defense Industry – Mitigating the Challenges." *Journal of Service Management* 21, no. 5, pp. 656–674.

Noordhof, C.S.; K. Kyriakopoulos; C. Moorman; P. Pauwels; and B.G.C. Dellaert. September 2011. "The Bright Side and Dark Side of Embedded Ties in Business-to-Business Innovation." *Journal of Marketing* 75, no. 5, pp. 34–52.

Ostrom, A.; M.J. Bitner; S.W. Brown; K. Burkhard; M. Goul; V. Smith-Daniels; H. Demirkan; and E. Rabinovich. February 2010. "Moving Forward and Making a Difference: Research Priorities for the Science of Service." *Journal of Service Research* 13, no. 1, pp. 4–35.

Parasuraman, A; V.A. Zeithaml; and L.L. Berry. Spring 1988. "SERVQUAL: A Multiple-Item Scale for Measuring Service Quality." *Journal of Retailing* 54, no. 1, pp. 12–40.

Pine, B.J. 1992. *Mass Customization: The New Frontier in Business Competition.* Boston, MA: Harvard Business School Press.

Prahalad, C.K.; and V. Ramaswamy. January–February 2000. "Co-opting Customer Competence." *Harvard Business Review* 78, no. 1, pp. 79–87.

Salas, J. 2013. *Replicating Hybrid Solutions for Business Customers: A Proposed Framework for Service Infusion Success.* (Order No. 3604994, Arizona State University). ProQuest Dissertations and Theses, 165.

Sawhney, M.; R.C. Wolcott; and I. Arroniz. Spring 2006." The 12 Different Ways for Companies to Innovate." *Sloan Management Review* 47, no. 3, pp. 75–81.

Sawhney, M.; S. Balasubramanian; and V.V. Krishnan. Winter 2004. "Creating Growth with Services." *MIT Sloan Management* Review 45, no. 2, pp. 34–43.

Sharma, D.; C. Lucier; and R. Molloy. 2002. "From Solutions to Symbiosis: Blending with Your Customers." *Strategy and Business* 27, pp. 38–43.

Stanley, J.E.; and P.J. Wojcik. June 2005. "Better B2B Selling." *The McKinsey Quarterly* 38, no. 3, p. 15.

Vargo, S.F.; and R.F. Lusch. May 2008. "From Goods to Service(s): Divergences and Convergences of Logics." *Industrial Marketing Management* 37, no. 3, pp. 254–259.

Vorhies, D.W.; and N.A. Morgan. January 2005. "Benchmarking Marketing Capabilities for Sustainable Competitive Advantage." *Journal of Marketing* 69, no. 1, pp. 80–94.

Wise, R.; and P. Baumgartner. September–October 1999. "Go Downstream: The New Profit Imperative in Manufacturing." *Harvard Business Review* 77, no. 5, pp. 133–141.

Index

Announcing the Business Expert Press Digital Library

Concise E-books Business Students Need
for Classroom and Research

This book can also be purchased in an e-book collection by your library as
- a one-time purchase,
- that is owned forever,
- allows for simultaneous readers,
- has no restrictions on printing, and
- can be downloaded as PDFs from within the library community.

Our digital library collections are a great solution to beat the rising cost of textbooks. E-books can be loaded into their course management systems or onto students' e-book readers.

The **Business Expert Press** digital libraries are very affordable, with no obligation to buy in future years. For more information, please visit **www.businessexpertpress.com/librarians**. To set up a trial in the United States, please email **sales@businessexpertpress.com**.

CPSIA information can be obtained
at www.ICGtesting.com
Printed in the USA
FFOW05n1219260714